MIGRANT TEACHERS

MIGRANT TEACHERS

HOW AMERICAN SCHOOLS IMPORT LABOR

Lora Bartlett

Harvard University Press

Cambridge, Massachusetts

London, England

2014

KH

Library of Congress Cataloging-in-Publication Data

Bartlett, Lora, 1967–
   Migrant teachers : how American schools import labor / Lora Bartlett.
      pages cm
   Includes bibliographical references and index.
   ISBN 978-0-674-05536-0
   1. Education, Urban—United States.   2. Teachers, Foreign—United States.   I. Title.
LC5115.B37 2013
370.9173'2—dc23   2013015284

9/8/15

To my teachers

CONTENTS

Transnational teacher migration first attracted my attention in 2004 when I was studying policy responses to problems of teacher recruitment and retention in England. Many of the schools I visited in the poorest parts of London were staffed primarily with South African teachers. The heads of these schools told me that they hired overseas trained teachers because they could not attract and retain native teachers. They spoke with respect and appreciation for the overseas teachers but also expressed concern about the transition challenges these teachers faced and the turnover inherent to their situation as temporary workers. I marveled at the trend and wondered about the effect on the school systems in both England and South Africa. So did others.

It was 2004, and the Commonwealth Education Secretaries had just met in Edinburgh, Scotland. A major topic of their meeting, and the subject of a subsequent policy white paper, was the challenge transnational teacher migration posed for developing countries. The policy conversation at the meeting sought to address the negative consequences for countries such as South Africa that struggled to staff their classrooms with qualified teachers. The meeting did not, however, even consider the possibly problematic aspects for the school systems of receiving countries. Both issues are important and worthy of scrutiny.

South Africa needs more teachers. Even without the increasing flows of teachers from developing to industrialized countries, the ongoing staffing problems there are gaining international attention. South Africa has a shortage of teachers in part because it has a shortage of adults, with so many lost to the AIDS epidemic, but also partly due to the outflows of teachers to other countries. The country has undergone massive changes socially, economically, and politically. The results of those changes include poorly organized infrastructures for public services, including schooling, low wages for teachers, and an unstable economy in general. South African teachers who sought and accepted work in England could secure higher wages and more stable working conditions—even if such employment lasted for only a few years. For many, this seemed to be a sensible individual solution. Such decisions, however, were negatively affecting the country's ability to meet the teacher workforce needs of their home country.

Meanwhile, England had a problem in recruiting and retaining teachers. Fewer people were entering the field, and half of those who did enter left before their third year of teaching. In response to the teacher labor market issues, policymakers debated whether to alter working conditions in a way that would increase workforce stability (for example, by expanding the population of paraprofessionals to support teachers), or to embrace a workforce model built on short-term participation and high turnover. In London, England's largest and most diverse city, the latter solution prevailed, at least in the short term, and South African teachers were part of the short-term transnational workforce solution.

All of this was interesting to me, yet seemed unique to the English condition. England and South Africa have strong colonial ties, and prospective teachers brought familiarity with a British system of education. That there is an annual meeting of the Secretariat of Commonwealth Countries Education ministers is testimony to this history and ongoing connection. The English system's practice of drawing teachers from developing countries to meet the needs of its teacher labor market seemed a fascinating but contextually bounded phenomenon. I was unfamiliar with this solution in any other industrialized country.

In 2006, while living and working in Northern California, I heard that officials from some local school districts were going to the Philippines to recruit teachers to fill posts they were unable to fill domestically. Intrigued by its similarity to the South-Africa-to-London story, I sought to learn more about overseas teacher recruitment in the United States. I looked first to the research literature and found almost nothing on the subject. I turned to district-level directors of human resources and found them initially reluctant to speak on the issue. The only real documentation that existed was in news articles in predominantly local papers. These papers reported the names of districts that were hiring overseas teachers and noted that many of the teachers were from the Philippines. That these hires were worthy of newspaper reporting suggested it was a new trend. I wanted to know more:

- How did the teachers come to be in the United States?
- Where are they working?
- Who are they?
- How many of them are there?
- How do they experience the U.S. schools?
- How do the U.S. schools experience them?
- What triggered this shift in hiring strategies?
- How successful is the experience for everyone involved— teachers, schools, students, and families?
- What are the implications for the teaching profession, the U.S. school system, and the school systems of developing countries such as the Philippines and South Africa?

I spent the next several years documenting the scope and pattern of teacher migration, exploring the experience of overseas trained teachers and the schools that employed them, and thinking about the implications for schools, students, teachers, and the teaching profession. What I learned is detailed in this book.

MIGRANT TEACHERS

"Everyone, please pay attention," calls out New Urban High School tenth-grade math teacher Alma Cruz.

Not a single student even pauses in conversation. Two girls at the back of the room are playing cards, a boy listens to his iPod so loudly everyone can hear it, and another boy is having a barely concealed cell phone conversation under his hoodie. A boisterous girl wanders from desk to desk making jokes and talking to friends. At one point, she grabs a boy's cell phone and takes a picture of herself with it. She flashes the image at other classmates and laughs loudly. Ms. Cruz carefully looks at no one in particular and repeats her request for attention.

She doesn't get it.

Actually, she doesn't really expect the full attention of her students. She proceeds, however, with her lesson as if everyone is listening. She stands determinedly by the overhead projector, carefully detailing the day's formulas and concepts. At the end of the day, she can check off another completed geometry lesson in the California state curriculum framework for a lesson no one heard.

Alma Cruz is an overseas trained teacher (OTT) brought to the United States to meet labor shortage needs in a low-income urban school. She is considered a highly qualified teacher by school district, state, and federal standards, with a preliminary California teaching credential, a master's degree in mathematics, an all-but-dissertation status in an education management doctoral program, and seventeen years of math teaching experience in the Philippines. This is her second year in the United States and at New Urban High School. Despite her education, experience, and credentialing, she feels ineffectual.

She is not happy with the students' inattention. In the Philippines, she taught classes of more than seventy students with great success. Here,

1

though, her hands are tied. She paid a lot of money to an international employment recruitment agency to get this job—three times her annual teaching salary in the Philippines—and she is in debt. Her family is still in the Philippines and is dependent on her for financial support. Retaining her position and her visa requires a positive principal evaluation. Such an evaluation requires her to be successful, with success being defined locally as getting through the curriculum and never sending a student out of her classroom unless she has been physically threatened. Her J-1 cultural exchange visa expires at the end of year three and she needs strong school-level support for the district to consider sponsoring her for the longer-lasting H1B work visa, a visa that might even make emigration possible. She has little power or support to get the students' attention, and they know it.

So she and the students have an unspoken agreement. They won't directly challenge her if she doesn't directly challenge them. A few of them tune in from time to time. Some of them may even learn something, as Ms. Cruz does know her material well. She glows when she speaks about the students who, in her estimation, "want to learn." She justifies ignoring the others as not allowing herself to be distracted by students who choose not to learn. She also acknowledges that she feels forced to choose between serving her students well and serving her family well. Alma Cruz is not alone in this dilemma.

Overseas Trained Teachers in U.S. Schools

Overseas teacher recruitment is a significant phenomenon in the United States. Alma Cruz is one of more than 90,000 OTTs sought by U.S. schools in the first decade of this century. Teachers such as Alma are recruited from the Philippines, India, Jamaica, Spain, and many other countries to teach in predominantly urban schools with the highest poverty student populations in America, school districts that have long been plagued with staffing problems. In the past, these schools have drawn on a secondary labor pool to meet their needs for teachers—namely, college-educated adults with little or no preparation to teach. Some of these "teachers" worked under temporary emergency licenses, while some were enrolled simultaneously in on-the-job training programs, and still others taught under a substitute teacher exemption. But none of them were fully qualified to teach.

The 2001 No Child Left Behind Act (NCLB) mandated that all schools employ teachers fully qualified in their subject areas or face federal school finance sanctions. School districts that did not meet federal requirements in this area would risk losing federal educational funding. This intensified the challenge for hard-to-staff schools by increasing the stakes of not employing fully qualified teachers. Intended to ensure that all students had access to fully qualified teachers, NCLB became an impetus for hard-to-staff schools to look to new markets for teachers. Many of them turned to the global market to find the teachers they needed, and the numbers of overseas trained teachers in U.S. schools swelled.

How large a trend is overseas trained teacher migration into the United States? As a percentage of the overall U.S. teacher population, OTT migration is insignificant. Ninety thousand teachers nationwide is a drop in the ocean compared to the 2.5 million teachers employed in the United States. However, the influx of OTTs seems like a tidal wave when compared to other alternative sources such as the nationally recognized internship program Teach For America (TFA). Furthermore, it is a highly significant portion of the labor market in the districts and schools that draw on the overseas market.

More overseas trained teachers have been sought to teach *in* America in the last ten years than there have been Teach *For* America teachers in the entire history of that program.[1] Modeled on the Peace Corps, Teach For America recruits recent American liberal arts graduates into a short-term teaching corps for hard-to-staff public schools. The program receives a great deal of research and public policy attention and many educators have debated its relative effectiveness at enhancing the qualified pool of teachers or improving the learning outcomes of students. In contrast to the more than 100,000 OTTs sought to teach in U.S. schools in a single decade, Teach For America recruited only 24,000 teacher corps members in two decades.

Although the numbers of overseas trained teachers are small nationally, they constitute significant percentages of the local teacher labor markets in certain cities. For example, between 2002 and 2008, New York City sought to employ more than 12,000 OTTs, and schools in two Houston, Texas, zip codes sought another 10,000 OTTs in the same time period. Those 22,000 OTTs make up nearly a quarter of all such teachers sought by U.S. school employers in the first decade of this century.

In high-poverty urban schools like New Urban High School, overseas trained teachers are even further concentrated in certain subject departments, comprising a third or more of math, science, and special education teachers in those departments. Alma Cruz teaches in a math department that is nearly 50 percent overseas trained Filipino teachers. The science department in her school is nearly 75 percent overseas trained Filipino teachers. In the math and science departments of high-poverty schools like New Urban High School, OTTs are increasingly the most significant source of teacher labor. Clearly, they are a labor source that needs to be better understood.

Schools and school districts seek overseas trained teachers with certain high-need subject specialism—most frequently math, science, and special education—to teach in the hardest-to-staff schools. District human resource (HR) specialists are clear that they restrict their overseas hiring to only the positions they feel unable to fill domestically. One school district human resource director offered this observation:

> Our goal was to bring over 100 math, science and special education teachers . . . We interviewed about 300 pre-screened teachers. (California HR director District A)

This sentiment was echoed in other school districts:

> I only hire international teachers when I can't find American teachers to fill the posts—like Speech Therapists and other special education teachers. (California HR director District B)

Others see overseas trained teachers as a resource for their district's harder-to-staff schools. Responsible for staffing large urban districts, these HR directors acknowledge that not all schools within their district are equally difficult to staff. They can address the challenge of the harder-to-staff schools with OTTs as well as other short-term labor solutions.

> Well, if you look at our district in general, some [higher poverty] schools are not so easy to staff. This year we made a concerted effort out of HR to staff those schools first. One of the things I haven't mentioned is Teach For America. We are very active with TFA, so we centered the international [teachers] and TFA on those particular schools this year. (California HR director, District C)

The movement to recruit overseas trained teachers emerged in the name of labor need. It did not arise from a quest for teacher cultural diversity or other benefits of international exchange. There is no national or cultural match between the student populations served and the teachers recruited to teach them. Overseas trained teachers are widely understood to be a short-term labor solution, a fill-in, a less desirable, and a temporary alternative to an American teacher.

> I think in everyone's heart, they don't think it [international recruitment] is here to stay. They think it is only here until we get enough Americans in Math and Science and Special Ed, to cover ourselves. (California District Administrator, District D)

But no one stated it more bluntly than the human resource district employee who, having hired hundreds of teachers on short-term cultural exchange visas, said:

> We're hiring these teachers because of labor shortage, not because we have a deep desire to build a cultural exchange with the Philippines. (California HR director, District E)

Interviews with human resource directors reveal repeatedly that OTTs are not their first choice. HR directors are not hiring them for the cultural diversity or exchange that they bring to schools, and they do not see overseas recruitment as a long-term labor market solution. Overseas trained teachers are one way that they can fulfill the federal requirements for teacher quality. School districts hire OTTs when they have to fill critical labor shortage areas in hard-to-staff schools for policy compliance purposes. District administrators sought and found a solution that let them meet the national standard. Many are conflicted about it. They know it is a short-term solution and many acknowledge limitations of the approach for schools, teachers, and students. But when American school district administrators need a math, science, or special education teacher that can meet the national subject standards, they know they can find those teachers in overseas markets.

An International, Invisible, and Underinvestigated Trend

Transnational teacher migration is not just an American trend. England hires overseas—and there are indications that other industrialized countries also look to developing nations for their teacher supply in much the same way nurses have long been recruited to work in industrialized nations.[2] In 2008, half of all teacher applicants in New Zealand came from outside of the country, and there are indications that South Korea hires Filipino teachers of English as a second language. These teacher migrations are many and varied across national borders.

Despite the growing scale of transnational teacher migration, little research documents these movements. What research exists tends to investigate teacher migrations in relation to the implications for developing nations. These studies operate from a position of presumed gain in the number of qualified teachers to industrialized countries based on the loss of these teachers from developing countries. Few studies consider the actual experience of industrialized countries as the receivers and hosts of overseas trained teachers and none have yet to consider the overall implications of a transnational orientation for the teaching profession.

The existing research on how developing nations are affected by teacher migration covers two main areas. First, it illuminates the existence and some patterns of teacher movements from developing to industrialized countries. Second, it highlights the complicated set of consequences of teacher migration for developing countries.

Guyana, Jamaica, and South Africa are among the developing countries that have identified teacher migration as a major struggle in meeting domestic and international educational goals. The 2003 Conference of Commonwealth Education Ministers in Edinburgh, Scotland, noted that while teacher migration presents benefits, primarily in the form of increased revenue for developing countries, such teacher migration could, at the same time, hinder the attainment of educational goals in those developing countries. A paper from this conference offered this information:

> There are patterns of movement between developing and developed countries . . . For example, there is movement to the UK from Commonwealth countries in Africa, the Caribbean, as well as Australia and New Zealand . . . There can be benefits to both individuals and countries from the effects of mobility. For developing countries, the outflows of skilled people can generate significant remittances, and longer-term benefits may include the new skills and contacts brought back by returning migrants. Movements can, however, also be a drain on human resources which are in short supply and which—when added to other factors resulting in teacher loss—may adversely impact upon countries' abilities to meet key educational goals and objectives,

including for developing nations, the Millennium Development Goals [which include achieving universal primary education and eliminating gender disparities in education].[3]

The education goals to which the ministers refer come from the Education for All (EFA) movement, coordinated by the United Nations Educational, Scientific and Cultural Organization (UNESCO) and aim for universal primary education. EFA goals include gender parity in primary and secondary education and a 50 percent improvement in worldwide literacy rates by 2015. UNESCO has identified insufficient numbers of qualified teachers as a major barrier to attaining EFA goals by 2015. It estimates that developing countries need to increase their teacher supply by 20 percent annually to attain the goal of universal primary education.[4] This estimate does not account for the migration of qualified teachers from developing to industrialized countries.

The Global Campaign for Education (GCE), an international agency with union and NGO membership from 150 countries, has prioritized teacher recruitment, retention, and development as the key factors in meeting EFA goals. GCE has launched an international campaign to increase the global supply of teachers by 15 million over the next ten years, and cites the loss of teachers in developing countries to industrialized countries as a barrier to increasing these numbers where they are most needed. Education International, an international federation of teachers' unions, addressed this issue in an article on the shifting of poor teachers to rich countries:

"They come back every year, and every time they come, we lose dozens of teachers," complains Evelyn Crawford, President of the Guyana Teachers' Union (GTU). "They" are the British recruiters on their annual visit to Guyana to meet teachers who replied to their advertisements for applicants to teach in Britain.

"Recruitment agencies from the United States and the Bahamas are now flocking in, too . . . Jamaica is another stop on the recruitment agencies' itinerary. Byron Farquharson of the Jamaica Teachers Association (JTA) estimates that 300 teachers leave the country each year. "Three hundred out of the 23,000 teachers in Jamaica might not seem much, but it is," stresses Byron, because "the teachers recruited are in fields where Jamaica has a shortage: maths and science. . . ."

"Industrialised and developing countries face the same shortages," notes Byron, "except that the industrialised countries have
a way out: take our teachers!"[5]

These reports and related research raise questions about the implications of teacher migration for teacher supply issues, teacher status, and
schools in developing countries. They tend not, however, to ask similar
questions for industrialized nations or for the teaching profession in general. The presumption seems to be that industrialized countries win at
the expense of developing countries. Industrialized countries "have a
way out" of the math and science shortages—that is, to take the best
teacher brains of developing countries and move them to schools in
industrialized countries. This "gain," however, is based almost solely on
assumption. There is very little published on transnational teacher migration that attends to the experience of the receiving schools and nations.

Attention to teacher migration into the United States is even more rare.
What articles are available suggest that there may be losses as well as wins
for schools recruiting overseas trained teachers, with research indicating
that these teachers are less effectual with students than U.S. prepared
teachers.[6] To be effectual, OTTs need specialized induction support to
guide them as they adjust to the differences in student population, school
workplace, and culture.[7] Despite the lack of research endorsement, overseas trained teacher recruitment has risen rapidly in the United States.[8]

Book Overview

This book is a systematic analysis of the experiences of teachers educated overseas, who have worked as teachers in other countries and then
migrated to teach in an industrialized country. It looks at how students,
schools, and teachers in the United States experience transnational
teacher migration and how the teachers themselves experience migration. While the scope and patterns documented here are national, the
qualitative and ethnographic work is focused on California,, which is
one of the major receiving states in the United States and offers an
insightful nested case.

This book finds that transnational teacher migration presents no
guaranteed win for industrialized countries—nor is there a guaranteed
loss. Whether or not transnational teacher migration constitutes a success for industrialized countries is dependent on teachers' reception into
the labor market and their effectiveness in the workplaces of the receiving

countries. All too often movements of teachers require teachers to rise to the top of the developing country's teacher labor market in order to ascend to the bottom of the industrialized nation's labor market. This book explores what it means for U.S. schools, for teachers, and for the teaching profession to have overseas trained teachers migrate specifically to teach in the United States.

The focus here is on documenting and exploring the phenomenon of the transnational migration of teachers and their experiences as a means of informing the wider international conversation, through the lens of the American experience. In particular, the book considers the flow of teachers into the United States from many different countries, both developing and industrialized, and pays particular attention to the experience of Filipino teachers who migrate to teach in U.S. public schools.

The story of teacher migration from the Philippines to the United States offers insight into all teacher labor migrations from developing to industrialized countries. It provides an empirically grounded case of teacher labor migration from which a more generalized understanding of this phenomenon emerges. The stories of teachers migrating from many different countries into the United States demonstrate the variation of teacher experience and the implications of teacher migration for schools, students, and nations. This book positions teacher labor migration in the broader political context of education and immigration policy, considers the effects of teachers' motivations and personal circumstances on migration experience, and accounts for local reception and framing of teachers in considering the experience of overseas trained teachers in the schools of industrialized countries.

The chapters that follow explore the phenomena and consider the efficacy of transnational teacher migration. They also consider the implications of an emerging new concept in an increasingly global world: the migrant teacher.

Part One: The Count, Context, and Conditions

Chapter 1, "The Scope and Pattern of Overseas Trained Teachers in U.S. Schools," presents national data as well as California state data to make the unequivocal case that the recruitment of OTTs to teach in U.S. schools is a growing trend concentrated in certain high-poverty urban centers. These data also highlight the primacy of the Philippines as a U.S., and especially a Californian, source of OTTs.

Chapter 2, "The Perfect Policy Storm: Colonization, Education, and Immigration," explores the immigration and education policy conditions that led to the rapid increase of transnational teacher migration into the United States—and the social and historical colonization context of these patterns. The chapter argues that the three elements of colonization, education, and immigration aligned to create a "perfect policy storm" resulting in a rise of OTT migration flows into the United States. Conditions for the storm converged when No Child Left Behind created demand for teachers with subject specialism and the expansion of the U.S. H1B labor visas opened the door for migration—and the century-old colonization of the Philippines made it a productive door to open.

Part Two: The Teachers and the Schools

Chapter 3, "Transnational Teacher Motivations and Pathways," offers a close look at what motivates teachers to migrate to the United States, the pathways that bring them here, and how these two factors shape the experience of overseas teachers in U.S. schools. There are significant differences between teachers driven to come to teach in the United States out of economic deprivation versus those drawn to an opportunity for travel, fun, and adventure. Further, teachers travel to their U.S. schools via different institutional pathways and those pathways affect their migration experience. In particular, teachers motivated to move from economic deprivation who travel a recruitment agency pathway are most likely to have climbed to the top of their home country's teacher labor market in order to migrate to the bottom of an industrialized country's teacher labor market. This dynamic sets up an unnecessary dichotomy—pitting teachers' income and migration goals against their ability to serve students well.

Chapter 4, "Navigating Migration," traces the variations in both how teachers position themselves for transnational migration as well as how they orient to the short-term nature of the visas. Some teachers pursue specific teaching specializations in order to migrate—while others are already well-established and experienced in high-need subject areas. Furthermore, some teachers embrace or adapt to the short-term nature of the visa, while others aspire to stay beyond the visa limits. These differences affect teachers' orientation to their work, position, and power in relation to their employment, and they have implications for both the quality of teachers' experience, the risk of exploitation, and the quality of teaching itself.

Chapter 5, "A Tale of Two Schools: The Transient School and the Transplant School," lays out the organizational context of the teachers' work and experience through the case studies of two high schools that represent two very different orientations to teachers and their work as well as two different realities for overseas trained teachers: the transient school and the transplant school. Transient schools become magnets for the least-empowered OTTs, framing them and treating them like short-term labor; in doing so, these schools practically ensure the teachers' failure to thrive. Transient schools hire teachers because they need someone—anyone—who meets the on-paper qualifications to fill a spot in a classroom. In contrast, transplant schools are both more appealing to teachers who are in a position to be selective and are generally more selective employers themselves. Transplant schools carefully choose each teacher hired with an eye toward building its faculty, and then invest in teacher development and retention. A transient orientation to teachers' work results in higher teacher turnover and lower student achievement. Of the two types of schools that employ overseas trained teachers, the norm is a transient orientation and the exception a transplant orientation.

Part Three: Implications

Chapter 6, "Teachers' Work," explores the reciprocal relationship between conceptions of teachers' work as involving low status, subject specialization focused on technical work, and the rise of transnational teacher migrations. That teachers' work is narrowly conceived and presumed to be decontextualized allows for the notion of a short-term, high-turnover teacher labor market. This short term labor market orientation contributes to the narrow conception of teachers' work and low status of the teaching profession. This chapter draws on the guest worker literature to better understand the experiences and positions of teachers in these migrations. It also looks critically at what the current teaching profession is and what it is becoming.

Chapter 7, "Transnational Teacher Migration," revisits the major themes of the book, highlighting the dilemmas of teacher migration, considering the efficacy of the practice, and addressing the implications for industrialized countries. It concludes that industrialized countries' framing and practices around OTTs determine the relative success of transnational teacher migration. Overseas trained teachers can be effective teachers in U.S. schools. Schools in industrial countries need to attract teachers who aspire to stay and create conditions that facilitate transplant. Industrialized countries are the driving force in the cultivation of what it means to be a transnational teacher—in fact, in what it means to be a teacher.

PART ONE

The Count, Context, and Conditions

1

THE SCOPE AND PATTERN OF OVERSEAS
TRAINED TEACHERS IN U.S. SCHOOLS

Overseas trained teachers (OTTs) are a growing source of U.S. teacher labor, particularly in the math, science, and special education departments of high-poverty urban centers. Urban school districts seek OTTs when the domestic American market fails them. They draw on the overseas market to staff the highest-need subject areas in low-income schools with teachers who meet the qualified teacher policy requirements.

The scope and pattern of OTTs in the United States is discernible through the collective analysis of immigration visa data and California state teacher credentialing data as well as through interviews with teachers, recruiters, and school leaders. In particular, data regarding the two most common OTT visas—H1B labor shortage visas and J-1 cultural exchange visas—highlight national trends. California state teacher credentialing data offers a window into the employment patterns of OTTs over a longer period of time and reveals each teacher's country of origin. From this analysis we can see the special case of the Philippines as a significant source of teachers for California schools.

Difficult to Discern

It is difficult to discern the scope and pattern of overseas teachers in the United States. Although schools and states report teacher ethnicity, gender, age, years teaching, credential status, and more—they are not required to report nationality or visa status. For one thing, teachers are recruited on multiple types of visas and the information available on those visas is minimal and variable. Many states collect data on country of teacher education in the credentialing process; however, that information is generally internal, unreported, and disconnected from place of employment

15

and visa type. Furthermore, many teachers are recruited by agencies and placed in schools throughout the United States. These agencies do not need to report their placement patterns.

There is no clear and simple visa for guest teachers as there was for farm workers during the U.S. Braceros program of the 1940sthrough 1960s, or as there is currently for foreign nurses today.[1] Instead, OTTs are mixed into a sea of labor-shortage visas—a pattern that is obscured through the use of cultural exchange visas. Finding the scope and pattern of OTTs using standard immigration or education reporting systems is like using a satellite map to try to identify the colors and styles of individual houses—you can, but it is time consuming and prone to error, and it requires further verification. Determining the scope and pattern of OTTs is thus a time-consuming process that requires multiple data sources in order to minimize error and ensure accuracy.

Documenting the distribution of OTTs requires accounting for teachers working on both H1B labor shortage visas and J-1 cultural exchange visas—neither of which is readily documented, though for different reasons.

The J-1 Visa

The J-1 visa is issued through the U.S. Department of State, which has this to say on its website about the exchange visitor program:

> The Exchange Visitor Program promotes mutual understanding between the people of the United States (U.S.) and the people of other countries by educational and cultural exchanges, under the provisions of U.S. law. Exchange Programs provide an extremely valuable opportunity to experience the U.S. and our way of life, thereby developing lasting and meaningful relationships.[2]

Designed to allow for cultural exchange, J-1 visas are generally issued for one year and are renewable up to two times for a maximum of three years. Only authorized agencies can host J-1 visas and they typically require evidence of a two-way cultural exchange. Many live-in nannies are recruited on J-1 visas: Their host agencies must ensure they attend classes that will enrich their experience in the United States, and the nannies must document how they share their home culture with the children in their care. Universities also often rely on J-1s for international scholars. The visa recipient, not the employer, pays the costs associated with a J-1 visa, which is predicated on the assumption and requirement that visa holders will return to their home countries to complete the circle of exchange. There is no annual cap on J-1 visas and the numbers and distribution of them is not readily available to the public. They are seen as a cultural exchange visa rather than a work visa and, therefore, they are not an issue related to the labor market or economy.

It was only through teacher interviews conducted for this book that it became apparent that many overseas teachers are recruited on J-1 visas and that these teachers and their visas are under the radar of any reporting mechanism. There is no current way to approximate the number of teachers working on J-1 visas in the United States or to determine their distribution. Most of the case study teachers in this book started on J-1 visas with the idea of converting to an H1B. The J1 visa must be sponsored by an agency with an established visitor exchange program as designated by the U.S. Bureau of Educational and Cultural Affairs. These agencies are responsible for ensuring that the visa conditions are met—including a two-year mandatory repatriation clause intended to ensure teachers return to their home countries to complete the circle of exchange and their time as a visitor. In order to be considered a visitor, a teacher must at some point go home—thus fulfilling the temporary status J-1 visa requirements.

There are a few exceptions, and some school districts have become known among the teachers as employers that offer longer-term H1B labor shortage visas. In California, however, J-1 visas are the most common initial teacher visas among teachers interviewed for this book.

The H-1B Visa

The U.S. Department of Labor offers this explanation for its H-1B program:

> The H-1B program allows employers to temporarily employ foreign workers in the U.S. on a nonimmigrant basis in specialty occupations or as fashion models of distinguished merit and ability. A specialty occupation requires the theoretical and practical application of a body of specialized knowledge and a bachelor's degree or the equivalent in the specific specialty (e.g., sciences, medicine, health care, education, biotechnology, and business specialties, etc . . .).[3]

Unlike J-1s, H1B visas are designed to enable employers to fill labor shortages by recruiting overseas. Many people are familiar with the H1B visa—but most think of it as a high tech or science oriented visa—one that employers such as Microsoft lobby to protect and increase in order to help ensure U.S. competitiveness in computer engineering. Congress does, however, designate approved labor shortage areas: education is an approved field and schoolteacher is an approved profession, though these regulations do not specify certain subject or grade level designations.

An H1B visa allows three years of employment and is renewable for a second three-year cycle. Although it is not an immigration visa, it is considered convertible because a visa holder can apply for a green card while working on an H1B visa. Subject to an annual cap set by Congress, H-1B visas are distributed in most years through a lottery process in April for October work start dates. The lottery is a competitive process, so receiving a visa is by no means a certain outcome. Renewals are exempt from the annual cap, as are employees affiliated with a university or other research institution. Actual H1B recipients, both employers and employees, are not reported publicly, making H1B scope and pattern difficult to definitively discern.

Although the number of teachers in the United States on an H1B visa is difficult to discern, this number can be approximated by analyzing the employer applications for U.S. Department of Labor condition certifications for positions they seek to fill with overseas employees. The Labor Condition Application (LCA) is the precursor to the H1B visa and has been required by law since January 2001. Seeking to certify a position with the Department of Labor signals interest and intent to seek an overseas trained teacher on an H1B visa. Getting the position certified authorizes the employer to seek the overseas employee and the H1B visa. It does not guarantee that the employer will find a suitable candidate, nor does it ensure that the U.S. Department of Homeland Security will issue an H1B visa. The visa is, of course, subject to the lottery. Because Congress requires this DOL labor condition certification process to be reported publicly, the data generated permit an approximation of the scope and pattern of overseas trained teachers in the United States. While not a perfect measure, it is the only current means of perceiving national patterns.

The national scope and pattern analysis that follows here is based on the Labor Condition Applications made for teachers and certified by the Department of Labor between 2002 and 2008. These numbers represent employer intent and interest to employ overseas trained teachers. They do not include teachers hired on J-1 visas, nor do they exclude LCAs that did not result in a successful hire with an H1B visa. Therefore, these numbers can be seen to both underreport and overreport the scope of OTTs in the United States, although they are most useful as a way of revealing patterns. Consequently, they are discussed here as "effort to employ" OTTs rather than as hires or actual teachers. The LCA numbers allow a look at which employers in what regions of the country and demographic communities sought to employ overseas trained teachers, and they reveal patterns clearly. Interest in overseas trained teachers is concentrated in high-poverty urban communities with schools that primarily serve low-income, nonwhite students for whom English is not their first language.

High Poverty Urban Concentrations

Between 2002 and 2008, U.S. public schools sought to employ 91,126 OTTs with labor shortage visas (H1Bs). Ten states captured 78,073 of those, and just three states—Texas, New York, and California—account for 57,187, nearly two-thirds of all OTTs sought nationwide. State population alone does not account for these concentrations. Even when teacher employment efforts are looked at in relation to the numbers of public school students per state, Texas, New York, and California still lead the nation. Although we would expect states with higher numbers of students to seek higher numbers of teachers, these states, even when normalized for student population size, still lead the nation in seeking to employ overseas trained teachers, as illustrated in Figure 1.1.

Texas leads the nation with 36,330 OTT searches initiated between 2002 and 2008—one-third of all searches nationwide, although it would be more accurate to say that Houston, rather than all of Texas, leads the nation in the number of OTT searches. Ten thousand such searches were initiated in just two central Houston zip codes, and the greater Houston area accounts for a third of all Texas searches. When Dallas, Austin, Waco, and the Mexican border area of McAllen are included, most efforts to employ OTTs in Texas are captured in these areas, as shown in Figure 1.2).

In New York state, the concentration of OTTs in impoverished urban areas is even clearer. If you are an OTT in this state, then you probably teach in New York City. While New York state school employers sought

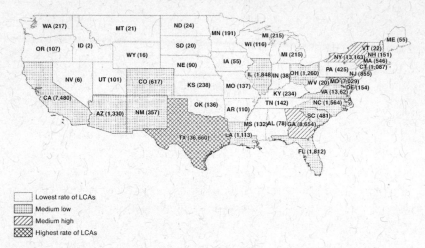

Figure 1.1 Number of teacher LCA applications by state, 2002–2008, normalized by public school student population.

13,131 OTTs between 2002 and 2008, New York City initiated 94 percent (12,374) of the searches. Ranking overseas teacher searches by state puts Texas as the leader, but ranking by urban centers puts Houston and New York City on equal ground.

The story is similar in California. The state has almost a thousand school districts but OTTs are not evenly distributed among them, being concentrated instead in just twelve high-poverty, low-achieving urban school districts. Twelve school districts account for 68 percent of the 7,438 H1B visas sought for OTTs in California between 2000 and 2006. These twelve school districts serve more than a million K–12 students, including about a quarter of the state's recipients of free and reduced lunches. Their student populations are predominantly nonwhite English language learners. In fact, in 2006, all twelve of the school districts where H1B visa requests were concentrated had fewer white students and more English language learners than the state average and, in ten of the twelve, free and reduced lunches were higher than the state average. The only area in which these school districts fell below the state average was in the percentages of fully qualified teachers employed. All twelve have historically depended on underqualified teachers to ensure adequate staffing numbers. These districts have had success in increasing their percentages of fully qualified teachers between 2001 and 2006—and OTTs are one way they have achieved this increase.

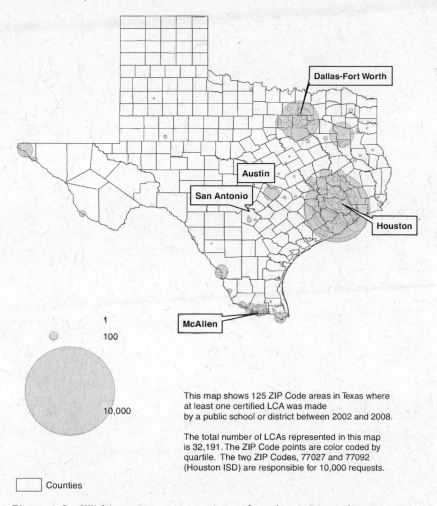

Figure 1.2 Within-state concentrations of teacher LCA applications in Texas (locations of major cities on this map are approximate).

California's District A, while an extreme case in terms of the sheer number of teachers it sought, is typical of employing districts in terms of its student demographics. Set in a city with a population of just fewer than 100,000, District A is home to roughly 30,000 K–12 students. In 2001, 99 percent were nonwhite, with one-third of those students African American and two-thirds Latino. Sixty-one percent were English language learners and 71 percent lived below the poverty level. District A served these students with 1,367 teachers—66 percent of whom were not fully qualified. While District A's student population changed little between 2001 and 2006, its teacher population altered significantly. The district reduced its percentage of unqualified teachers from the 2001 high of 66 percent to a 2006 low of just 27 percent. During that same time period, District A had 1,379 teaching positions certified by the U.S. Department of Labor as meeting the conditions for an H1B labor shortage visa. If each of these job certifications resulted in a person with a visa, District A could have replaced every one of its teachers with an OTT who met the state credentialing standards. In fact, interview data bears out that District A did draw heavily on the overseas labor market in altering its workforce composition. According to Eduardo Ferraro, one of the many overseas teachers recruited to District A from Spain, "District A hired hundreds of Spanish teachers . . . and then they switched for a time to Mexico, and now they are probably recruiting Filipino teachers."

Eduardo's exchange was facilitated by a formal agreement between the California Department of Education and the Spanish Ministry of Education. Aware that other U.S. states also participate in the exchange that helps school districts meet their teaching needs, he explains the process:

> It's an Education Exchange Program between the Ministry of Education of Spain at the National Level and . . . many States through[out] the nation, from North Carolina to Washington to California, which is one of the biggest ones—California, Texas, and some of the East Coast States. Other ones, like Maryland of all places, they were recruiting a lot of Spanish teachers at one time because of the bilingual need and they thought that the qualification of the Spanish education degrees was pretty good for this.

As Eduardo's awareness of the agreements between the Spanish government and U.S. education agencies suggests, District A is not alone in seeking OTTs. These districts are working to address their need for teachers who meet the requirements for fully qualified teachers. All but one of the twelve California districts saw marked increases in their percentages of qualified teachers during the time period they actively sought OTTs.[4]

Hiring OTTs for Math, Science, and Special Education

Our interviews with overseas trained teachers indicate a concentration in math, science, and special education. Occasionally, we encountered a

Spanish-language teacher, but most OTTs we met in California—and we met more than 200 in the course of the study—taught math, science, or special education.

The LCA data suggest that this focus on math, science, and special education recruitment overseas is a national one. The job title field on the application form is open-ended. Some employers are very specific—indicating, for example, that they are seeking a ninth-grade algebra teacher. Most, however, tend to be vague and specify only general categories like "teacher," or perhaps "secondary teacher" or "primary teacher." The ones that do specify a subject or pedagogical specialism, however, indicate a search for math, science, and special education teachers as well as language teachers, both foreign languages and English as a second language. Of 91,410 positions sought between 2001 and 2009, more than 20,000 were specified as math, science, and special education, while language posts made up 17,460 and the remaining 53,936 were captured in general and unspecified teaching categories (see Table 1.1). Given the district level reports we heard and the OTTs we met, the likelihood is that a large percentage of the more than 50,000 unspecified teacher searches were also in math, science, and special education.

Taken together, this means that overseas trained teachers are concentrated in the math, science, and special education departments of the hardest-to-staff schools in the highest-poverty school districts of the United States.

And this is only what we can see. There is much that is still obscured to our view.

An Increasing Trend

The certified teacher LCA numbers reveal a slight decline between 2002 and 2003, followed by a generally increasing trend of the recruitment of OTTs (see Figure 1.3). What is not clear, however, is how these numbers relate to earlier flows of OTTs. It seems possible that, like nurses, teachers have been a steady, unobserved labor migration into the United States. Because the LCA data do not allow for a pre-2002 analysis, a national approximation is not possible. However, there are indicators that the recruitment of OTTs is a new and growing trend. Seventeen years of California credential data indicate an increase in OTTs earning state teaching credentials from an incidental to a noteworthy percentage. Some states have only just started seeking to employ OTTs, suggesting a "catching on" of the practice.

Table 1.1 LCAs by year and position type, 2001–2009 (N = 91,410)

Year	Math	Science	Foreign language	ESL bilingual	Special education	Primary	Secondary	General teacher	Other
2001	12	12	24	35	38	58	53	54	2
2002	288	213	1,225	3,579	1,224	2,457	2,316	1,355	31
2003	228	167	399	1,184	1,231	3,462	2,037	1,598	222
2004	331	231	298	3,064	1,578	2,137	2,417	1,629	63
2005	472	389	339	1,126	1,602	2,522	2,100	2,351	50
2006	677	837	523	1,539	1,919	3,702	2,541	1,754	109
2007	794	727	427	1,705	2,612	2,942	1,801	5,054	170
2008	1,102	691	394	1,587	2,519	3,298	1,947	3,414	107
2009*	4	2	1	11	114	71	104	2	6
Total	3,908	3,269	3,630	13,830	12,837	20,649	15,316	17,211	760

* 2009 data are partial and incomplete.

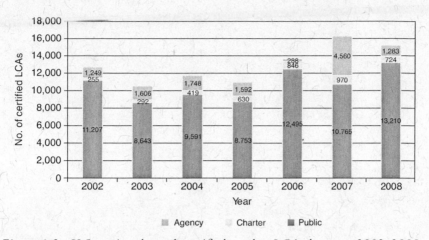

Figure 1.3 U.S. national trend certified teacher LCAs by year, 2002–2008. (*Source:* http://www.flcdatacenter.com.)

California has collected data regarding the country of a teacher's education on its credential applications since 1991. Overseas trained teachers were credentialed in California pre-2000, but the numbers were low and the countries of origin numerous. Since 2000, however, these data reveal a clearly increasing trend. The flow of overseas teachers into California accelerated greatly after 2000, peaking in 2002, and the number of OTTs from 2003 to 2006 has continued to be significantly higher than it was before 2000 (see Figure 1.4). In California, 7,589 OTTs were credentialed between 1991 and 2006—however, 62 percent of those credentials were issued between 2001 and 2006.

Not only did credentialing of OTTs peak in 2002, but teacher credentialing in general peaked in California that year. Overall state credentials issues went from 22,122 in 2000 to 23,926 in 2001, to a significant step up to 29,536 in 2002. The 1,200 OTTs credentialed that year, up from 600 in 2001, correspond with the 1,417 LCAs sought by California school employers that year, giving credibility to the relationship between LCAs certified and teachers in U.S. schools. At 4 percent, it is still not a large proportion of teachers credentialed in relation to the statewide numbers. However, given the fact that these teachers are principally employed—as the LCA data indicate—in twelve California school districts, then OTTs emerge as a significant localized labor market solution for these communities. Starting in 2002, the global market became a significant source for some localized California labor markets—and, by

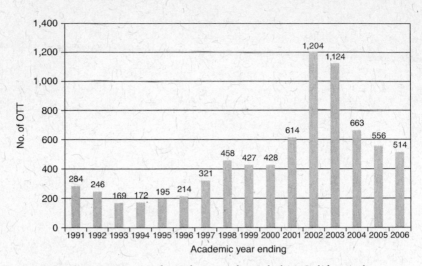

Figure 1.4 Overseas trained teachers credentialed in California by academic year, 1991–2006. (*Source:* CCTC-OTT data, 03/2007.)

extension, for the United States. Other states caught on to the potential of the global market only by extension. Maryland is a perfect example.

In 2002, Maryland was not a significant player in the global teacher labor market—at least not as indicated by its participation in the H1B LCA process. In 2002, Maryland schools sought to certify only 130 teaching jobs with the U.S. Department of Labor; however, those numbers more than doubled to 443 in 2003, and then jumped repeatedly again to 811 in 2006, and to 1,612 in 2007. In 2008, the state sought labor certification for 3,147 teaching jobs—a twenty-four-fold increase in annual numbers in only six years. These ever-increasing steps into the global teacher labor market signal a rapidly changing orientation to sources for teachers, a growing awareness of and appeal to OTTs. Furthermore, as elsewhere around the country, Maryland searched for OTTs to fill positions in high-poverty urban districts: in particular, 2,417 of the 3,147 teachers sought overseas in 2008 were for only two school districts—in Baltimore and Prince George's County.

In Maryland, as elsewhere, OTTs are framed as a staffing solution for high-poverty schools. Prince George's County School District clearly identifies hiring OTTs from the Philippines as a part of its strategy to improve the percentage of "highly qualified teachers" in low-income public schools, to be more in alignment with higher-income schools. In its 2006 master plan document, Prince George's County Public Schools recognizes that it had already hired 80 teachers from the Philippines, and states its intent to "hire 107 certified teachers from the Philippines to be placed in high-poverty schools with vacancies" (September 2006).[5]

Maryland is a major draw for teachers from the Philippines, and many of them interviewed can generally name one friend from home who ended up there, and many also sought jobs in Baltimore or Prince George's themselves. Teacher interviews alone reveal a great deal about the scope and pattern of the ever-expanding Filipino teacher diaspora. From those conversations, it is clear that although Filipino teachers may be found anywhere in the United States, they are most definitely concentrated in Maryland, Texas, North Carolina, and, of course, California. Furthermore, these teacher interviews highlight the newness of the trend. Many of the interviewed teachers report that their awareness of opportunities to migrate to the United States started in 2001. That was when they started to see their colleagues leave to teach in America.

Teacher Sources: The Growing Primacy of the Philippines

As the numbers of California's OTTs have changed, so has the primary source of those teachers. Although California OTTs come from 114 different countries, twenty-three sending countries account for 75 percent of the sixteen-year total, and six countries account for 59 percent—the Philippines (22 percent), Canada (12 percent), Spain (11 percent), India (7 percent), Mexico (4 percent) and England (3 percent). Russia and Australia each supplied 2 percent of the total, and fifteen other countries each supplied 1 percent. None of the remaining ninety-one countries provided even 1 percent of the total (see Table 1.2).[6] While cumulative percentages indicate the overall supply of teachers between 1991 and 2006, the order of those countries as top annual suppliers, as well as the cumulative positioning, has shifted over the last sixteen years. For example, although the Philippines has supplied almost a quarter of all OTTs over the entire time span, as of 2001, it had supplied only a tenth of all OTTs. And although Canada and Spain were for many years the largest annual suppliers of OTTs, by 2006, Canada had fallen to second place and Spain was fifth, supplying fewer than either India or Mexico. During the 2002 and 2003 peak credential years, the Philippines provided 29 percent and 36 percent respectively, and, although the

Table 1.2 National sources of California OTTs by number and percentage, 1991–2006

Country	Total number	Total percentage
1. Philippines	1,652	22%
2. Canada	936	12%
3. Spain	838	11%
4. India	508	7%
5. Mexico	306	4%
6. England	246	3%
7. Russia	188	2%
8. Australia	124	2%
9. Nigeria	105	1%
10. Germany	80	1%
11. Taiwan	80	1%
12. South Africa	73	1%
13. Korea	70	1%
14. Ukraine	67	1%
15. Peru	63	1%
16. Armenia	59	1%
17. China	52	1%
18. Chile	48	1%
19. Argentina	47	1%
20. Japan	46	1%
21. Colombia	43	1%
22. Bulgaria	42	1%
23. Ireland	38	1%
Subtotal	5,711	
Unknown origin	987	13%
Other 91 countries	891	12%
Total OTTS, 1991–2006	7,589	100%

Source: California Commission on Teacher Credentialing-OTT 03–07.

overall numbers of OTTs were down in 2006, the Philippines supplied 37 percent of the year's total.

From 1991 through 2001, Spain and Canada supplied California with the largest numbers of OTTs, both annually and cumulatively. The other top four countries trailed far behind these top two sources. However, in 2001, the number of OTTs coming from the Philippines equaled the numbers coming from both Canada and Spain. In 2002 and 2003, the peak credential years in California overall and for OTTs, the

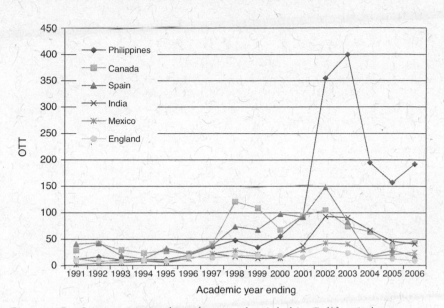

Figure 1.5 Overseas trained teachers credentialed in California by year and country. (*Source:* CCTC-OTT data, 03/2007.)

Philippines leaped ahead of all other sources; by 2006, the Philippines was the undisputed primary source of OTTs in California for that year and, cumulatively, between 1991 and 2006 as well (Figure 1.5).

Between 1991 and 1997, no single country supplied more than fifty teachers annually to California. In 1998, the number of OTTs from Spain and Canada increased significantly over the number of OTTs who came in prior years and from other countries; the number from Spain went from 38 in 1997 to 74 in 1998, and the number from Canada increased from 41 to 121. In 1998, Canada provided 26 percent and Spain 16 percent of that year's OTTs (see Figure 1.6). For Canada 1998 was the peak year in both annual numbers and percentage of supply of OTTs to California. Although Canada maintained its position as the top overall supplier (see Figure 1.7) until it was equaled by the Philippines in 2002 and surpassed in 2003, Canada's numbers and annual supply share declined steadily until the point that it supplied only 9 percent (46) in 2006. For Spain, 1998 was part of an increasing supply pattern that topped out in 2002 at 148 and 23 percent of the year's supply, before beginning a marked and rapid decline down to only 18 teachers and 4 percent of the year's OTT credentials.

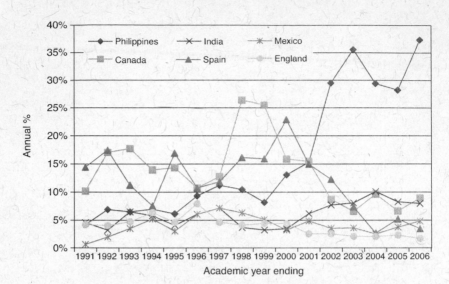

Figure 1.6 Annual percentage of new OTTs credentialed in California, by country of origin each year, 1991–2006. (*Source:* CCTC-OTT data 03/2007.)

While the annual supply of Canadian and Spanish teachers declined, the Philippines supply increased consistently as an annual and cumulative percentage. In 2001, the three countries were essentially tied as the top supplier, with each providing 15 percent; however, in 2002, the Philippines leaped to 29 percent of the total (355 teachers) and, while the numbers of OTTs from the Philippines have fluctuated some, dipping in 2004 (195) and 2005 (157), the Philippines has since provided no less that 28 percent (2005) of California OTTs annually, with a high of 37 percent (192) in 2006 (charts annual percent and cumulative percent).

The raw numbers of OTTs from the Philippines in California in 2004 and 2006 are essentially equal, at 195 and 192 respectively, but they represent different annual percentages of market share, at 29 percent and 37 percent respectively. This is indicative of the declining numbers from other sending countries and the increasing primacy of the Philippines as a supplier of OTTs in California. Given the relatively minor role the Philippines played in overseas teacher supply between 1991 and 2000, this sudden change in overall numbers, and annual and cumulative percentages is worthy of notice and exploration.

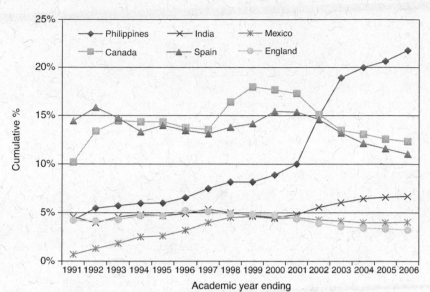

Figure 1.7 Cumulative percentage of all OTTs credentialed in California, by country of origin, 1991–2006. (*Source:* CCTC-OTT data 03/2007.)

In Sum

A sudden change in 2002 seems to mark the real start of a significant global teacher labor market in the United States. During that year, the overseas trained teachers credentialed in California spiked up, and during the following six years, cities such as Houston, New York, and Baltimore turned increasingly to overseas sources of teacher supply to fill their teaching positions. The experiences of individual teachers, the credential patterns of overseas teachers, and the department of labor visa process data together strongly indicate a new and growing global teacher labor market trend: one that draws teachers from one of the globe's poorer nations to teach in the poorer school districts of an industrialized country such as the United States.

In 2002, education demand for subject-qualified teachers, coupled with immigration supply increases, all set against a backdrop of historical colonization, came together to create the perfect policy storm of transnational teacher migration into the United States.

2

Colonization, Education, and Immigration

"Actually, before 2001, I think there really wasn't any buzz in the Philippines that they were in need of teachers here in the United States. It was more nurses, IT people that were coming in the 90s. It [the demand for teachers] just came on in the 2000s."[1] The "buzz" this Filipina teacher refers to accompanied the increase in overseas trained teacher flows into the United States—its echo in the streets of Manila, Cebu, and other areas of the former U.S. colony. The conditions were perfect for a rapid expansion of teacher labor migration from the Philippines to the United States. American public schools needed teachers who could meet the new national subject specialist requirements, immigration law had created expanded pathways for labor migration and, a century ago, American colonization set the scene for the Philippines to be a good source of teachers for American schools.

The federal government passed the No Child Left Behind Act (NCLB) in 2001, which sought to address educational inequity and increase student achievement by ensuring that all teachers were "highly qualified." High poverty school districts—which had long been staffed with emergency credentialed teachers—were the target for these reforms. The resulting changes in the teacher workforce indicate the policy focus hit its mark, at least in part. School districts had to take teacher qualifications—as defined by NCLB—seriously. All teachers had to be subject specialists. In fact, subject specialism is the primary emphasis of national policy definitions of teacher qualifications, and districts were on the lookout for ways to increase the percentage of their teachers who met these clear standards.

At the same time, Congress lifted long-held caps on the annual number of H1B visas from the traditional 65,000 to 105,000 annually in 1999 and 2000, and then increased the number again to 195,000 in

2001, 2002, and 2003. In 2004, the visa cap returned to its previous norm of 65,000 annually. This increased availability of H1B visas corresponds with the 2002 rise in overseas teachers nationally and particularly in California. This suggests that the availability of labor visas helped spur the rise of overseas teacher recruitment. Although not all overseas trained teachers are working on H1B visas, the increase still seems to have signaled to agencies and employers an opportunity to tap new overseas labor markets.

The Philippines offered a fertile source of overseas teacher labor and a labor market accustomed to overseas placements. The Philippine economy is dependent on salary remittances from its overseas Filipino workers (OFWs), who are celebrated as national heroes. Their income makes up 12 percent of the Philippines' gross domestic product. Furthermore, its K–12 school system was established and modeled on the U.S. school system, including the use of English as the primary language of instruction. The two nations' educational systems share more, however, than a language of instruction. The division of instruction by age and subject matter, and the teacher education requirement of student teaching and subject specialism are also related. Although, arguably, there are as many differences as similarities between the two systems, the two are structurally and linguistically compatible and the colonial links between the two create a pull for Filipino teachers in search of increased status and income.

When Filipino teachers migrate to U.S. schools, they experience a pay increase of more than thirteen times their annual salary. The average monthly home salary of Filipino teachers is $364. Contrasted with their monthly U.S. salary of more than $4,900, the economic incentives are clear. Calculated in annual terms, that is $4,400 versus $59,400.[2] Reports from U.S. school districts suggest that there are more than ten qualified applicants in the Philippines for every U.S. teaching position posted, and Filipino teachers talk of the professional status gained from their time teaching in the United States in addition to the financial benefits to their families.

The three elements of colonization, education, and immigration have aligned to create a "perfect policy storm," resulting in the rise of overseas trained Filipino teacher flows into the United States. The seeds of the storm were sown years ago during the U.S. colonization of the Philippines, which was followed by the NCLB's demand for teachers with subject specialism and the expansion of the U.S. H1B labor visas.

Each of these elements deserve greater attention to fully explicate the complexity of the situation and the way these elements have come together to facilitate transnational teacher migration.

Colonization: The Roots of Migration

In the years following the Spanish-American War, the United States practiced an intentional policy of empire expansionism and colonization in the Philippines, setting out to "Americanize" the Philippines by remaking the country in its image. Establishing both a health care system and an educational system based on U.S. models was a large part of that initiative. To "uplift and civilize" the Filipinos through "benevolent assimilation" was an essential strategic function of creating and cultivating a system of public education in the Philippines.[3] In 1900, President William McKinley appointed William Taft as head of the Philippine Commission, which came to be known as the Taft Commission. The commission functioned as the legislative branch of the Philippines under the sovereign control of the United States between 1900 and 1916. McKinley prescribed three key elements needed before self-rule could be restored in the Philippines: public education, economic development, and democratic government. In January 1901, the Taft Commission took a big step toward the expansion of education when it passed Education Act Number 34, establishing the Philippine Department of Public Instruction. This department was charged with creating a universal system of public education in English that built on the earlier initiatives of the U.S. Army begun during the Spanish-American War.

To export American education required the export of American teachers. In July 1901, 530 American teachers set sail from San Francisco for Manila Bay upon the *U.S.S. Thomas* to establish the Philippine education system. A year later, more than 500 additional American teachers joined them. They became known as the Thomasites, after the ship that brought the first large contingent of teachers, and they worked with a missionary zeal. The Thomasites spread out across the archipelago, opening schools, cultivating teacher education colleges, and spreading the use of English. By 1909, the number of elementary schools in the Philippines had tripled and the number of students served doubled. American teachers led the crusade to make the Philippines the most literate country in Southeast Asia.[4]

The practice of importing American teachers to the Philippines tapered off as more Filipino teachers were prepared domestically. In the first decade after the arrival of the Thomasites, the supply of native teachers tripled and, over time, the system's emphasis on academic over vocational education led to an abundant supply of both teachers and nurses. Whether that supply was excessive or not is both a debatable and debated question. Certainly, the flow of nurses out of the Philippines and across the globe started early in the century and has continued until today.[5] Some credit the outflow of teachers as a fortunate result of excess supply; others report that the outflow has led to teacher shortfalls that contribute to increasing class sizes, reduced quality of instructors, and a growing trend to out-of-field teaching.[6]

The early twentieth century colonization of the Filipino educational system laid the groundwork for the transnational migration of teachers to the United States. A century later, the Philippines makes for fertile teacher recruitment ground, as it shares English as its primary language of instruction, is built on a U.S. educational model, and its well-developed public education system nets a large percentage of well-educated citizens. Perhaps as important is the way teaching in the United States continues to be perceived as a source of status and opportunity among Filipinos. Just as Filipino nurses have long sought out U.S. career and education opportunities as a means of leveraging their career, so now do teachers. Whether they stay in the United States for the higher salaries and improved lifestyle or return to the Philippines with the status advantage of having worked and possibly gained education in the United States, Filipino nurses and teachers expect to improve their life circumstances and their professional standing through their U.S. work experiences.

Changes in both immigration and education policy created a pull that tapped into the Filipino teacher supply—and the flow spiked in 2002, when more OTTs were credentialed in California and more U.S. districts sought labor condition applications for OTTs than any year prior or since. The confluence of increased demand for fully credentialed teachers created in 2001 by the NCLB legislation, together with the 2001 increase in congressional caps on H1B visas, seem to have created the conditions for the "perfect storm" of the rapid expansion of the global teacher labor market in California.[7] NCLB created the demand and the visa cap increase allowed for teacher entry from other countries, especially the Philippines.

Education Policy: The Quest for Qualified Teachers

The 2002 OTT peak coincides with the No Child Left Behind Act (NCLB), which was signed into law in January 2002. In addition to mandating that states adopt federal academic standards, develop an aligned assessment system, and set annual student achievement benchmarks, the policy included federal mandates about teacher qualifications. The stated purpose of NCLB is threefold:

1. To improve teacher and principal quality and,
2. To hold schools accountable for student academic achievement, thereby
3. Increasing student achievement.

NCLB mandates that schools employ highly qualified teachers (HQTs), which it defines as ensuring subject expertise. This national policy attention to teacher quality and qualifications is just one more step in an ongoing professional and policy orientation to teacher quality. Ensuring an adequate and evenly distributed supply of well-qualified teachers has been a focus of school reform policy for more than half a century. That teachers "matter" is an established point—but how they matter, what constitutes adequate educational preparation, the dimensions of necessary subject and pedagogical knowledge, and the significance of experience is contested.[8]

The current policy and research position, as embodied in the NCLB, defines highly qualified teachers principally as having subject expertise. It emphasizes defining and determining the individual characteristics of well-qualified teachers and focusing policy attention on improving those qualifications and their distribution. There is a documented maldistribution of teachers in the United States who are defined as "well qualified," with an inverse relationship between teacher qualifications and student poverty, English language learner status, and low achievement rates.

The NCLB teacher quality movement has made progress toward highlighting and correcting that maldistribution. For example, in California in 1999 and 2000, four times as many teachers in the state's poorest public schools were underqualified as in the state's wealthiest public schools. In 2002 and 2003—only one year after NCLB had passed—the likelihood that students in high-poverty schools were being taught by an underqualified teacher dropped from four times to less than three times as likely as students in higher income schools.[9] Although this is still grossly inequitable, it is a significant improvement realized in just one year.

No Child Left Behind highlights subject expertise but excludes other dimensions of teacher quality, including capacity to serve as a conduit to cultural capital, ability to attend to the social and emotional development of children, ability to adapt pedagogical practice, and familiarity with the local context or awareness of culturally relevant pedagogy.[10] All are elements associated with effective teaching practice.

The NCLB emphasis on subject knowledge privileges this type of knowledge in definition, as well as expectations of teacher quality, without accounting for cultural knowledge of American society and the local community, or knowledge of pedagogical practice. It has spurred the creation of state-level teacher tests to ensure teacher subject knowledge and increased attention to the subject matter preparation of teacher education programs and school hiring practices that emphasize subject matter over all other elements. Subject knowledge, pedagogical knowledge, and subject pedagogical knowledge have long been accepted as essential elements of teacher quality.[11] The problem is not what this definition of teacher quality includes—but rather what it excludes. Teaching work, many contend, is not decontextualized or simply technical. In other words, being a good teacher requires more than subject matter knowledge.

Essentially, NCLB's definition of qualified teachers as possessors of subject expertise sets the scene for districts to import teachers from other countries on temporary work visas. If the main work of teachers is to convey academic subject content, and the definition of highly qualified is one who possesses subject matter knowledge, then a subject specialized teacher from any context at a school for any amount of time fulfills the quality requirements. NCLB's Title II provision for highly qualified teachers paved the way for overseas teachers in U.S. schools by creating demand for subject specialists without attending to other dimensions of teacher and workforce quality.

Immigration Policy

The 2002 peak also corresponds with changes to congressional H1B visa caps. Traditionally capped at 65,000 new visas annually, Congress raised the cap to 105,000 in 2000 and increased it again in 2001 to 195,000, where it stayed until returning to the 65,000 cap in 2004.

The rise and fall of H1B visa caps correspond with the rise and fall of OTTs credentialing rates in California, suggesting a relationship between federal immigration policy and the supply of qualified teachers in California. The rate of OTTs in California has increased over the last sixteen years. Between 1991 and 2006, 7,589 OTTs were credentialed in California. Thirty-eight percent (2,914) of those awards occurred in the first ten years, with 62 percent (4,675) awarded in the most recent six years, and a peak in 2002 of 1,200 credentials. This 2002 peak makes sense given the NCLB policy focus on increasing the number of well-qualified teachers in public schools starting in 2001, and represents the tendency of some schools to look overseas to replace positions previously filled by teachers considered underqualified.

As detailed earlier, districts and schools are clear about their reasons for looking overseas for teachers. They needed to meet the NCLB highly qualified teacher standards and OTTs offered an efficient and accessible solution. The increased H1B visa caps opened the schoolhouse door to the global teacher labor market, creating an increased supply opportunity. Although H1Bs are most often associated in the public mind with engineering, computers, and technology jobs, they are also accessible to teachers and schools. Teachers, as designated by Congress, are one of the U.S. labor shortage categories.

H1B visas are labor shortage visas intended to allow American employers to hire overseas workers to fill labor market needs not being met by domestic labor. While they do not disallow applications for permanent residency, they also do not guarantee any rights to remain beyond the three-year visa, renewable once for a maximum of six years. Employers and immigrants seeking to extend a worker's stay beyond that six-year period must be granted permanent residency. Marriage to an American citizen, evidence that employment is in the national interest, or proof that a worker is not readily replaceable in the workplace are all grounds for permanent residency—but residency is certainly not ensured. Furthermore, the demand for H1B visas often outstrips supply, resulting in a lottery allocation process that further limits the reliability of the H1B visa.

Recruitment agencies played a significant role in making the connection between the teacher qualification demands on NCLB and the opportunities of immigration visa quota changes. The nursing migration infrastructure was positioned to quickly mobilize when the need for teachers became apparent. Many of the first teacher recruitments were facilitated by agencies long accustomed to moving nurses between the

38

Philippines and the United States—whose names reflect references to health care, medicine, and nursing These agencies are not a surprising source of teacher labor for U.S. schools if the context and history is understood. Some newspaper articles have claimed to trace the increased teacher migration from the Philippines to California back to one nursing recruitment company in Southern California that saw the opportunity in increased H1B visas and the teacher labor market. Universal Recruitment, according to a 2001 *Los Angeles Times* article by Joe Matthews, is owned and operated by the Henrys—a couple with ties to the Philippines and a successful history of nursing recruitment. They worked with Compton and other nearby districts to recruit Filipino teachers, the first of whom arrived in 2001:[12]

> Compton, a struggling district that only recently emerged from an eight-year state takeover, was desperate for qualified teachers— particularly in math and science. In the spring of 2001, Compton officials, working with the Henrys, took a recruiting trip to the Philippines. At one interview site, a line of 300 applicants stretched around the block. By May 2001, the district had made offers to 58 teachers. They all accepted. (*LA Times*, August 10, 2002)

The Henrys were inspired by news of Compton's need for teachers and felt confident in their ability to bring Filipino teachers to the United States permanently—rather than on a cultural exchange—and at no cost to U.S. schools. No Child Left Behind created the demand and the increase in H1B visa caps created a visa opportunity. Other companies also reported the H1B visa as an initial draw to the teacher labor recruitment market. While the H1B clearly piqued recruiter and employer interest in overseas trained teachers, it failed to deliver fully on its early promise as a pathway to permanent U.S. teacher employment.

Although H1Bs opened the gates to increased interest in and flows of OTTs, there are significant ways in which the H1B visa has failed to meet the labor market needs of U.S. schools. The uncertainty of the lottery and the visa quotas are challenges that are further complicated by the timing of the visa allocations. Although the lottery takes place in April, visas do not take effect until October 1—a date that misses the start of most traditional school years by a month or more. H1B visas are thus limited, uncertain, and inconvenient for schools.

Schools and recruitment agencies, frustrated by failed lottery applications and late starts, sought a more flexible and reliable alternative. The

J-1 visa quickly became a popular alternative. As a cultural exchange visa, the J-1 is intended to allow short-term cultural exchanges between the United States and other nations. Unlike the H1B, it does not require labor condition certification by the Department of Labor as it is premised on the notion of cultural experience rather than labor shortage. Consequently, it is a shorter-term visa than the H1B. Other news reports indicate recruitment agencies moved to J-1 visas as a more reliable source of visas and that many teachers believed this could and would translate into H1B visas. Consider the example of Melba Cayme—whose story is reported in a March 2004 article in the Philippines Inquirer News Service:[13]

> Like 59 others who left Manila three years ago, Filipino teacher Melba Cayme is wracked with anxiety about her future. Cayme, 57, came to the United States on a J-1 trainee visa[14] and, through Health Quest, a Filipino job placement agency in Missouri, got a job as a science teacher in Jamaica High School here. The New York Board of Education currently pays her 6,000 dollars a month. But her contract will end on Sept 9, the day her J-1 visa expires . . .
>
> She said she and her colleagues, some of whom had found teaching jobs in California and Pennsylvania, were planning to overstay in the United States and wait for the conversion of their visas from J-1 (for trainees) to H1–B (for workers).
>
> But in the meantime, they will be jobless because of the "no visa, no job" policy in most U.S. public schools.
>
> Each teacher had paid Health Quest 2,500 dollars to find a sponsor for their H1B visas but the agency failed to do so, Cayme said.

In this way, J-1 visas, often billed as a first-step visa, actually end up as the only visa of many OTTs in the United States. Of course, many such tales are heard again and again when talking with OTTs: stories of teachers hoping to get H1B visas, stories of teachers changing employers in order to be in school districts suspected of being good visa sponsors, and stories from school district personnel acknowledging how infrequently they actually elect to sponsor a J-1 visa teacher for an H1B visa. These stories suggest that the numbers of teachers working on J-1 visas may far outstrip the numbers of teachers on H1B visas. This furthers the argument made in Chapter 1 that, in all likelihood, labor condition applications—the precursor to the H1B—underestimate the number of OTTs in the United States.

Other Sources of Overseas Trained Teachers

Of course, not all sending countries are former colonies of the United States. Canada and Spain are both in the top three sources of sending countries for California's OTT credentialing and neither is a former U.S. colony. Between 1991 and 2006 Canada provided 12 percent and Spain 11 percent of all OTTs credentialed in California. In contrast, the Philippines provided 22 percent (see again Table 1.2). The Filipino lead, however, is primarily accounted for by its dramatic increase in 2002. The annual number of Canadian and Spanish OTTs did increase slightly between 2001 and 2002 but not to the same extent as the 2002 increase in Filipino teachers (see again Figure 1.6).

Changes in U.S. immigration visa policies as well as the NCLB increased demand for qualified teachers, created new opportunities for teachers from all sending countries to migrate to the United States. That the increased supply response was not similar across source countries indicates that not all sources were as affected by increased opportunity. Migration motivations, a topic explored more in Chapter 3, vary across individuals but also by country of origin. That the numbers from Spain and Canada did not spike suggests that the reasons to migrate had less to do with opportunity than they did for teachers from the Philippines. As a former colony of the United States, the Philippines and its teachers are very differently positioned than teachers from either Spain or Canada. Although the contrast case of Spain and Canada cannot completely confirm the role of colonialism in teacher migration, it does offer some reinforcement to the argument.

In Sum

The confluence of increased demand for fully credentialed teachers created by NCLB legislation with the 2001 increase in congressional caps on H1B visas together created the conditions for the "perfect storm" that contributed to the rapid expansion of the global teacher labor market in the United States. Colonization laid the groundwork for the recruitment of teachers from the Philippines in the early part of the twentieth century through the formation of a public education system created in the image of the U.S. system. NCLB created the demand for OTTs, and the visa cap increase created a supply. The United States then drew on the results of those systems in the early part of the twenty-first century in an effort to address its own teacher labor shortage.

PART TWO

The Teachers and the Schools

3

TRANSNATIONAL TEACHER
MOTIVATIONS AND PATHWAYS

The numbers, origins, and concentrations of overseas trained teachers sought in the United States since 2002 provide little more than an outline image of the teachers—a shadow. These data indicate little to nothing about who they are, why they have come, how they got here, and what they experience. It does not reveal their feelings, struggles, goals, hopes, and motivations. To truly see the teachers requires conversation with, and observation of, the teachers themselves. To capture the teachers' stories for this book required spending a great deal of time with teachers in the schools, classrooms, and places they call home while they are in the United States.

The stories of overseas teachers compiled and shared here come from interviews with fifty OTTs conducted in California between June 2008 and August 2009. Some of the teachers had been in the United States for as little as a week, and others, up to fifteen years. Observation data included following two dozen Filipino teachers through their first two weeks in the country and gathering related information from the job fair placements, classes, teacher social events, professional development, department meetings, and personal conversations they experienced during this time. The teachers were very generous with their time, stories, and trust. From this research, some commonalities emerged around motivations, pathways, and experience.

These common threads offer a close look at what motivated teachers to migrate to the United States and the pathways that brought them here. The combination of motivations and pathway experience shapes the experience of overseas teachers in U.S. schools. There are, for example, significant differences between teachers seeking to come to teach in the United States to escape from poverty versus those drawn to an opportunity for travel and adventure.

Teachers who migrate from poverty are disadvantaged in their quest for work and their chances of a successful migration. They are also the teachers most likely to end up with the fewest opportunities to be effective in their new teaching assignments.

Teacher Motivations to Migrate

Understanding motivation for teacher migration is important for many reasons. It tells us about the elements that may affect the supply of teachers from various places, but, more importantly, it influences how teachers engage with their work, their personal and professional expectations, and their agency both individually and collectively. Asked how they came to migrate, the teachers interviewed offered two main motivations. One was migration from deprivation, disadvantage, and sometimes oppression; the other was migration toward adventure, lifestyle opportunities, or a better climate. In general, teachers' migration decisions can be divided into a *from* category and a *to* category. These categories mirror the push and pull factors traditionally considered by labor market theorists and made more robust in recent theoretical additions to the field.[1] Both *from* and *to* factors are always at work in any migration, and yet, one is often foregrounded. Most relevant in the case of teacher migration is the way the primary motivation positions teachers in relation to their work. Teachers migrating *from* something exercise much less influence on where they migrate *to*—taking a more fatalistic approach to their destination. Whereas, teachers migrating *to* something are much more discriminating and particular about their destinations, to the point that they will forgo migration rather than accept a destination that does not meet their preferences.

Migrating *From*

I only have one reason [to migrate from the Philippines]. That is the salary . . . the salary here is much, much better compared to the salary in the Philippines.

Maria Cruz speaks for herself, yet similar words were spoken by most of her fellow Filipino migrant teachers. As a thirty-eight-year-old math teacher with sixteen years of teaching experience, an advanced degree in her subject area, and two young children plus a husband whom she supports in the Philippines, Maria embodies closely the profile of the "typical" Filipino teacher in the United States in terms of age, gender, teaching experience, family situation, and motivation. Twenty-five of the thirty-three Filipino teachers interviewed are female—with an average age of thirty-nine and a median of thirteen years of teaching experience prior to migrating. Seventeen of the twenty-five women[2] are mothers who left children behind in the Philippines in order to teach in the United States. Like the others, Maria increased her annual income from $2,000 to over $60,000 a year. Her husband, a former jitney driver whose pay was about equal to hers as a teacher in the Philippines, has stopped working to provide child care to their children, aged eight and ten. Their children's private school education, household expenses, and more are now fully supported by Maria.

Similarly, Liezel Salvador migrated "for the future of my kids . . . for their college tuition." The private school tuition for her four school-aged children was $3,500 annually, while her annual income grossed just $4,000. College would cost even more, she knew, so she had to take steps to make provisions for their future. After fifteen years of teaching, the last five of which saw her in a key curriculum and guidance leadership position in her school, she decided to abandon her doctoral program in education to pursue a master's in special education. The latter, she knew, would enable her to pursue a teaching position in the United States at a salary that would make college a realistic option for her children, all currently under the age of fourteen. The day after she completed her special education degree, she signed a contract to teach in California. Within a few months, she had moved her children in with their grandparents, left the country, and accepted a position as a special education day class teacher in an urban middle school. This move increased her salary to more than $60,000 a year, enabling her to fund her children's current education, save for their future university costs, subsidize her sister's university studies, and sponsor fifteen scholarships for her former school employer. In addition, she covered the living expenses of her children and compensated her in-laws for housing them.

Before her migration, Liezel and her family lived on her teacher salary and her husband's slightly larger income. Combined, this income allowed them to keep their home and afford some other basics. Her American teacher's salary, however, made educational opportunities possible for their children. Both private school and higher education were now affordable options.

Many of the Filipino teachers indicated that their teacher salaries back home put them under national poverty levels—leaving them to work paycheck to paycheck. A bit of bad luck would leave them looking for loans and help from friends and family to make it to the next paycheck.

Alma Cruz, whose chaotic classroom opens this book, is migrating from poverty. She explains that "$400 (monthly) is not enough, so at the middle of the month, I'm just thinking where can I get the next money to provide for my family. I need a loan from a person, from my sister, and then—from the government." Taking loans put her behind each month, forced to start each pay cycle by paying off debts incurred in the subsequent month. It is a debt cycle that pushes many out of the Philippines:

> Oh, I never dream of going to the United States because I love my country, though it is poor, though it is hard to live in our country because we're not getting much in pay—it is really small pay. Because we cannot have everything in our life that we need . . . you cannot support a family [on a teacher's salary] . . . So, when I am in school during Saturday, when I am doing my PhD, one of my classmates told me, hey Alma, I want to say goodbye, I'm going to go to New York. And we were surprised because we never know that he is applying for New York. But he is also a Math teacher. And then, we were surprised and then he told me 'don't worry, just follow me. I'm going to wait for you'—and then, he gave me the phone number of the [recruitment agency].

Alma wants to be back home with her family. As a U.S.-based teacher, she supports her husband and two children as well as her mother, disabled brother, and his wife and children. She even built her brother a new house, as his former house routinely flooded. Her preference is clear though: if it were an option, she would go home and live simply without extras. She says, "If I am going to be receiving [monthly] like 50,000 pesos is like $1,000 here, I won't leave [the Philippines]." The 50,000 pesos she would like to be paid as a teacher in the Philippines is less than 20 percent of her U.S. salary—but more than three times what she has ever earned annually as a teacher in the Philippines. What she wants is a livable teachers' wage in her home country. What she has to choose between is a poverty-level income as a teacher in her home country or a comparably astronomical salary as a guest teacher in a foreign country.

The migration *from* stories are dominated by the economic imperative. The desire for economic improvement is a powerful factor in pushing teachers from some developing countries. The thirty-three Filipino teachers interviewed all cited economics as a primary motivation. Many never even considered leaving the Philippines until they learned of the U.S. income opportunities. For some, personal economic crisis preceded the move, while for others, the desire to improve their general standard of living fueled their migration.

There are, however, other reasons teachers gave for migrating *from* their country. Most notably, some of the female migrant teachers from both India and the Philippines gave migration reasons that could best be described as escaping personal or social oppression. Examples of this include the Indian widow who sought to escape the social ostracism she experienced after the death of her husband, a situation that positioned her socially as a symbol of bad luck:

> My life is a little different because, you know, in the mean course of time, I lost my husband, okay? So in India, our culture is entirely different. You should watch some of the movies. A single lady is always looked down on, and there is a lot of superstitious things that a widow is a bad omen for them.

Preetha Sunder, a high school chemistry teacher, found she could not raise her young son in the community where she was known as a widow. Other women would cross the street when they saw her approaching rather than encounter her. She sought migration as a way to escape this uncomfortable situation. She considered England, Australia, and the United States, and ended up in the United States because it was the first tangible opportunity to present itself. She trusted in God, she said, to show her the way forward.

Other examples of moving away from social oppression include another Indian teacher who moved away from social pressure to marry and the judgments she faced for resisting marriage. A Filipina teacher escaped an unhappy marriage by migrating to the United States in order to get a divorce, which was illegal at home. Another teacher left the Philippines to escape the racism that plagued her and her children for their mixed Chinese and Filipino heritage.

Although these teachers also migrated *to* something—to economic opportunity, to personal freedom, to acceptance—the desire to escape *from* something at home was the driving source of their motivation. For example, the Filipina teacher seeking a divorce also sought economic improvement—but only as it related to the independence she needed to obtain her divorce. And the single Indian teacher wanted a more socially liberal environment and was seeking to leave more conservative social expectations behind. These women, in all cases from developing countries, sought teacher migration opportunities as a pathway to personal, social, and economic empowerment.[3]

Teachers migrating *from* exert little influence on where they end up. The general attitude is to take the first position offered. Like Preetha Sunder's move to the United States over Australia and England, the decision is made on timing rather than destination. The goal is to move *from* something; the *to* matters less than the chance to migrate. Many of the Filipino teachers interviewed were placed in geographically dispersed school districts in states such as Maryland and Texas before ending up in California. They sought to migrate from the Philippines to the United States, but they did not generally seek to influence the choice of their destinations in specific ways. Furthermore, once in California, the teachers were similarly indiscriminate about the schools that became their workplaces. They typically accepted the first position offered to them, usually based on little information and without having ever visited the school.[4] They felt an urgency to secure a position—any position. They lacked viable options at home.

Their willingness to work anywhere was just what was needed by many of the school districts. In the case of the twenty-four newly arrived Filipino special education teachers, their lack of institutional status was clarified to the teachers early in their stay. At the orientation for newly arrived Filipino teachers, a district employee, herself a Filipina woman who had migrated many years before, welcomed them with the words "In the Philippines, you may have had servants. Here, you are the servants."[5]

She later explained that she wanted to help them understand their subservient role within the schools lest they think they had the right to be demanding about placement and working conditions. As new and hopeful immigrants, she said, they needed to not act entitled.

The teachers were told that the district brought them over to fill the harder-to-staff schools, and those were the schools that they directed the teachers to for interviews and placements. Positions that came open in schools higher up the local status ladder were not made available to these Filipino teachers. This was partly a function of when they arrived. The J-1 visa cohort arrived in August—a time when most schools still seeking teachers were the ones American teachers had bypassed. Yet, the district also intentionally filtered the higher status posts away from the overseas trained teachers based on the assumption that the local labor market would fill those posts. These preferences were articulated clearly and in multiple ways to the teachers. They were shown maps indicating where they could teach and, conversely, where they could not teach, and they were denied interviews at some schools based on the school's location and demographics. They were funneled toward the school districts' hardest-to-staff schools.

The overseas trained Filipino teachers got the message. They were at the bottom of the California labor market. They understood that there were some schools that were not for them and even some teaching subjects that were off-limits. Their need to get and keep a job, their lack of viable alternatives—their need to migrate *from*—put them at a disadvantage in their positioning within the local California teacher labor market.

Migrating *To*

Some teachers are motivated primarily by migration *to* something. For example, the teachers interviewed from Spain may have come to California to teach, but if living or working conditions proved unsuitable, they could readily return to the stability and certainty waiting for them in their home country. These teachers migrate *to* the United States for travel and exploration. Their teaching credentials function as passports for an extended working vacation. Most of them have teaching posts waiting for them at home, and their earnings in Spain are equal to or greater than their U.S. compensation. Economic gain is not part of their motivation. If anything, they are disadvantaged economically by their transnational migration as they often work at lower salaries and may lose some seniority accrual back home. They are not looking to migrate permanently. For the most part, Spanish teachers are younger than the Filipino teachers, often partnered but without children. They are stepping briefly out of their secure civil servant jobs at home for a bit of travel and adventure. Their transnational migration to teach is an option rather than a need, and while sometimes based on personal professional goals, it is consistently seen as rescindable at any time.

Marta Pinero, a thirty-three-year-old math teacher in her second year teaching at an urban U.S. high school, explains the situation:

We have the [teaching] position in Spain. We work for them forever, for the government, so we are safe on that way. For me like I
saw the public announcement about this and I felt "Why not?"
I can take a lot traveling . . . it's not a question of improving [money]
because I have a better job in Spain. It's a question of knowing
another culture, enjoying a new country. This was an adventure.

Married with no children, Marta has four years of teaching experience in Madrid. Like the other Spanish migrant teachers interviewed,
she came to the United States for an adventure, an extended holiday, and
an opportunity to travel. Her secure civil service job is waiting for her at
home with, according to her, better pay and working conditions.

I don't have anything to lose. It's like you keep your position and
Spain is going to be there forever and if don't like it here, I can,
you know, I can call and say I want my teaching job back. One
teacher already did it.[6]

When Marta speaks of her time in the United States, it is with a voice
of certainty and self-direction. She made a decision to spend some time
traveling and having an adventure. When the costs start to outweigh the
benefits, then she will return home to her secure position and resume
life there.

This quest for global adventure, coupled with a confidence born of
security, is typical of the teachers from Spain. Like Marta, they are primarily in their early- to mid-thirties with an average of five years of
teaching experience. They are usually partnered but not parenting. Their
partners always accompany them—right from the start. They look
incredulous when asked if they would still have come if their partners
were not also granted visas. They are mostly on temporary three-year J-1
cultural exchange visas, but they are not particularly concerned with
securing a means of extending their stays. In fact, like Marta, they are
not sure they will remain for the entire time permitted by the visa. Home
is always an option, and an appealing one.

Fernando Martinez, a thirty-two-year-old math teacher, had already
disrupted the norms by moving away from his hometown to teach elsewhere within Spain. He explains:

In Spain, there are not so many people that go out. Spain is so different from the States in that aspect. In Spain, most of the people

try to work in the place where he was born and where he has studied. Not all the people want to move and they don't want to go anywhere . . . There are a lot of people—if you are from a town, you want to stay in that town near to your family and near to your mother because most of it we are a matriarchal society. But for me, I feel I need to move. I need to make different thing. I need to change.

Many of the Spanish teachers expressed similar sentiments about being different, not only from other teachers, but from other Spaniards. Like Fernando, they considered themselves more open to relocation, and more desirous of travel and of experiencing other places and people far from home. Just the act of teaching abroad for a few years has, according to many of the teachers, marked them as different from other Spaniards, both less traditional and more adventurous. When Fernando talks about moving "out," he doesn't just mean from Spain—he means from one's hometown.

Aurora Ruiz, a thirty-four-year-old Spanish language teacher, credits her move as a teenager *within* Spain for giving her a taste and confidence to travel.

The fact that I moved from the North to the South of Spain when I was 15, I think, that made me less of a rooted person . . . I learned to survive in another city where I didn't know anyone. So you develop certain traits—your personality develops in those years—and I think I realized that I enjoyed meeting people. I mean, at first it was hard, but then I think that made me more brave and made me want to go to other places and meet other people . . . after university, I wanted to see the world.

Aurora has actually never taught in Spain—though she did return there for the interview to teach in the United States. Having set out after university to "see the world," she traveled and taught in several other countries. Teaching was indeed her passport. Spain's intensive teacher exam and the promise of a lifetime position lacked appeal for her. She wanted variety, travel, and freedom—not stability, certainty, and rootedness. A couple of countries into her teacher travels, she married. Her husband, an artist, is not Spanish or American, and his career does not lend itself as well to visas for foreign work, but Aurora's teaching skills have opened national doors for the two of them. They intend to stay the full three years of her visa, if possible—but they are also willing to move on sooner if that preference develops.

Alexandro Jorge de Balboa broke his mother's heart when he accepted a position teaching Spanish in the United States. She told him he was making a terrible mistake and giving up everything that was important—family, home, stability. She thought he should have considered himself blessed. At thirty-two years old, he was well established as a ten-year veteran language arts teacher at the same school he had attended as a student. According to his mother, he was respected in his hometown and should instead have been looking to marry and settle down even further. Alejandro, however, wanted a chance to travel, to live in another place, to do the very thing he told his students they should do:

> One of the most important things in life is to have the chance to travel abroad—to live in a different country, not on holidays. Because on holidays, the perspective is different, but if you have the chance to live there for a while, and for several months, in a way you grow as a person. It opens up your mind and [you] become a more enriched person.

There has been no mistake in Alejandro's mind, in part because he has nothing to lose. Life, as he sees it, is about personal choices, and this choice cost him little. He was in his first few weeks in the states and had not yet secured a position within his district—and yet he felt confident it was going to work out well. "I am one hundred percent sure that I made the right decision . . . I consider myself as a very lucky person to have the chance of being here while still keeping my position in Spain. I think, I think it's going to be a good year for me."

The confidence displayed by the teachers from Spain stems partly from their strong sense of personal choice and control. They are not in debt and can return home anytime. They will not accept teaching posts they don't find suitable. They didn't sell property or borrow money to get here, and no one back home is depending on them for financial support. They aren't even bothered if they don't end up earning full teacher credentials in the United States because they don't intend to stay. This position of power and agency is apparent in how they approach their work. All of the Spanish teachers spoke of the characteristics they required in a school and teaching position and none were prepared to accept a position at a school that did not suit them personally or professionally. Alejandro highlights this when he describes two recent school site visits as night and day in contrast with one another:

> I've just been in two high schools yesterday, and it was just, umm, night and day. We went to this high school; one of the biggest of the country, with more than five thousand students, and it was like a prison. It was probably the saddest place I've ever seen in my life. To be honest, I'm like, "oh my God." I mean, if I had to work in a place, you know like that, it looks like a jail . . . it was, I don't know if pitiful is the right word but umm, it was a sad place to be . . . : and then the other school was the other side of the card. And the most amazing thing was . . . the other school was just twenty-five minutes away from the other one. And uhh, this was a handsome school with large windows, lights everywhere, a beautiful campus. And there was no tension. When I went to the first school, you can feel from the vice principal or in the air, you can feel like a sort of a tension, you know? The second school, like any other place, was a friendly place.

Alejandro seeks a school somewhere between the two. He wants a place where he is needed, but also a place that will not fully consume him. He plans to spend more time enjoying himself while he is here, time doing things that one would do on holiday: ride a bike, go to the beach, and travel.

> I'm a teacher, and I want to be able to teach, you know. I haven't come all the way part from Spain just to babysit, in a way, you know? But uuhh, if I have to deal with a group of students who have difficulties, I'm ready to take the challenge and I'm really looking forward to taking it. But you know, I wouldn't like to be taking this sort of challenges you know, five hours in a row, every day. I would like to teach *and* do other things.

So, what if Alejandro's only option is the tense, troubled jail-like school? He recognizes the "chute to the bottom" that migration could lead to and has no intention of taking a post at the bottom of the American teacher labor market. He also knows he will opt out if necessary. If he is unable to find a school that suits him, he says he will cut his stay short and return to the work, school, and life he left on hold in Spain.

Rita Valdez feels the same way. As another teacher from Spain, she has taught Spanish and English as a second language for ten years. She also visited and interviewed at the schools Alejandro refers to as night-and-day different. Rita describes them as "hell" and "heaven," and is clear that she will not teach in hell:

> I want to work in a good school, I don't want to be—yesterday we had interviews in hell and heaven . . . I said to myself "I'm not going to work in hell." . . . Hell is a very run down area, very poor area. I have never seen anything like that school. I would have never imagined that in the first world country, there could exist a secondary school like that. Schools where children have to be fed in the morning for breakfast and for lunch—this is shocking for me.

Heaven, Rita says, was a beautiful school with manicured grounds and fountains. The atmosphere was peaceful and quiet and the students were happy and wanted to learn. The principal told the visiting Spanish teachers that there were no behavioral problems, no violence, and classroom management was not an issue at the school.

Alejandro was offered and accepted a teaching position at "Heaven." And while he, Rita, and other Spanish teachers were offered a position at "Hell," they all turned it down. The rejected school, however, did employ many OTTs from the Philippines. It had, in fact, one of the largest concentrations of Filipino teachers in the region.

Certainly, there are reasons other than the search for adventure that have motivated OTTs to migrate *to* the United States. Some mention an interest in learning new pedagogical practices to advance their professional knowledge, and others a search for a different lifestyle than that offered in their home countries.

Canadian teachers in California cited their desire to move *to* a better climate. Although the sample size was small (six OTTs), all of them cited a search for sun as their reason for relocating. They had made what they considered to be a permanent move with a labor shortage visa leading to resident status. They weren't fleeing anything at home—except perhaps long winters—and they didn't perceive teaching in the United States as offering them any added economic, professional, or status advantage. This is likely to differ for Canadians in other parts of the United States, though it isn't clear how large a migration they might make up nationally. It is clear that in California, Canadian teachers are in the top six for migrant teacher source countries and climate seems a big draw.

When teachers are drawn to migrate to a teaching opportunity—be it for reasons of global adventure or even climate—they are differently positioned than teachers who migrate *from* deprivation or oppression.

When returning home is a viable option, teachers approach their migration experience from a place of power and self-determination. They do not occupy the bottom of the California teacher labor market because they will not allow themselves to be placed there. Their motivation positions them differently on the migration pathway.

Migration Pathways

Migration pathways are the routes teachers take into U.S. schools and the way they navigate the journey. They have implications for the circumstances under which teachers end up working and their overall experience of migration. The institutional paths that bring teachers to the country have marked differences in the cost to teachers, the rights the teachers enjoy, and the overall experience of teacher migration.

Most school districts do not need to go along institutional pathways looking for overseas teachers; rather, the teachers are brought to them. This is true even in cases where school districts send employees overseas to interview teachers for open positions. The option of overseas teachers almost always appears on the district doorstep, so to speak. There are three main institutional pathways that lead OTTs to the doorsteps of American schools: from teachers themselves seeking employment, from government programs, and from private recruitment companies. Most OTTs are recruited and placed by for-profit recruitment agencies.

Individual migration draws the fewest teachers; government programs bring in more, but still in small numbers, while the private companies account for the numbers and rapid expansion into overseas labor markets.

Individual Migration

Sometimes a teacher draws on knowledge and networks to find American public school employers, acquire a work visa, and get cleared for a preliminary teaching credential. While there are very few of these teachers, there are some from almost every source country. All Canadian teachers interviewed had navigated this pathway themselves; however, only the most cosmopolitan and connected teachers from developing countries appeared able to manage a self-guided teacher migration. Those that did typically had prior travel experience as well as family or close friends already living and working in the United States.

These self-guided teachers are few, and although their stories are interesting individually, they offer little in the way of an institutional understanding of the migration patterns of OTTs.

Formal Government Programs

Formal government programs exist between some U.S. states and the governments of other nations; such is the case between California and Spain. Almost all of the Spanish teachers interviewed were recruited through this formalized government program.

Every year, a representative from the California State Department of Education journeys to Spain to interview prospective teachers who have applied through the Spanish government program. These teachers report having learned of the teacher travel opportunity through advertisements and postings on staff room walls, in teacher newsletters, and even on the evening news. They first submit an application that is then screened by the Spanish agency that, in turn, refers the teachers to the California Department of Education. All the teachers selected for an interview also take an abbreviated version of the state's teacher test. The teachers interviewed about this test all gave a similar account, and none seemed particularly stressed by the process. They knew they needed to have a few years of teaching experience and be able to demonstrate subject knowledge and English language proficiency to be selected. While the steps were clearly defined, none of the OTTs reported them as particularly daunting, nor were there reports of stiff competition.

The Spanish teachers did complain about the cost of the employment process. While there was no placement fee, they were expected to pay for the visa processing, translation of their academic records, and travel costs. In general, the Spanish teachers reported that migration cost them about $3,000 each. Notably, all of the teachers interviewed paid the costs from personal finances, and none of them borrowed money or sold anything to raise the funds. Also, because this is a formal government program, the teachers' jobs in Spain are held for them while they teach in the United States so that they may resume employment upon their return.

The two countries collaborate on the government program, which is intended to enrich both educational systems culturally rather than address a labor supply issue. Spain holds the teachers' positions for their return, with teachers returning with new pedagogical practices and stronger English language skills. California seeks more native Spanish speakers in its classrooms to enhance the experience of its primarily South American and Central American English language learners.

The program is small in scale, especially in relation to California's size, with fewer than a hundred teachers coming into the state from Spain each year on J-1 cultural exchange visas. The California State Department of Education is the official visa sponsor and the teachers are able to turn to a state government-based advisor and advocate when they need assistance. No individual or agency is profiting from this pathway. The teachers pay a modest sum for travel and processing in relation to their incomes, and the school districts pay nothing. Everyone involved—from the teachers, to the schools, to the facilitating government agencies—assumes that the teachers will return to their home country.

The pathway led by private recruitment agencies is a very different story.

Recruitment Agencies

Recruitment agencies sit between teacher and employer, between supplying and receiving countries. Typically, they are simultaneously recruiting teachers and courting U.S. public school employers. They identify school districts known to have recruitment and retention problems—mainly high-poverty, urban school districts—and offer to help them hire qualified teachers from other countries. The agencies facilitate the whole process—from advertising for and prescreening the teachers, to flying the U.S. human resource directors to the source countries for teacher interviews, to overseeing the visa application process, to arranging teacher travel and arrival in the school district. Generally, the agency also serves as either a visa sponsor or it subcontracts this requirement to an affiliated agency.

Agencies are the commercial conduits through which most Filipino teachers interviewed came to the United States. In the case of the Philippines, many of the agencies were originally formed to facilitate nurse migration, and their corporate names often reference the medical profession. Diversification into education and teaching seems to have occurred when agency leaders began to hear news reports of No Child Left Behind teacher quality labor needs in 2001 and 2002. With rare exceptions, these organizations are for-profit and their existence depends on a continual and steady flow of teachers from source countries to the United States.

Agency's are compensated either through teacher placement fees or as a percentage of the teacher's annual salary. Sometimes both. Teacher-paid placement fees are sizable in relation to the expense borne by teachers from countries like Spain and significant in relation to the home income of Filipino teachers. Those Filipino teachers who migrated from 2002 onward all reported paying between $8,000 and $10,000 to secure their American teaching positions.[7] Such costs included multiple placement fees as well as visa, travel, and other assorted expenses. Recall that the Spanish teachers paid only $3,000 in fees. The average Filipino teacher salary is $3,000 a year—less than a third of the cost to secure a U.S. teaching position. Some agencies are able to keep teachers on their payrolls and hire them out to school districts as temporary or provisional workers. In this way, the agency also collects a percentage of the teacher's salary. This fee model, although not found in California through our interviews, is in place in other parts of the country.[8]

All of the Filipino teachers who came through the agency pathway report the same experience of being selected from a large pool of applicants. Their experience evokes a chutes and ladders metaphor—meeting a series of challenges to move up each rung, with each step met by ever-decreasing numbers until only the teacher elite remained poised at the top of the ladder. These stories were so much the same that in interviews they felt like echoes after hearing them for the twelfth or the twenty-fourth time, and they all followed the same pattern:

- The first rung: Filipino teachers applied to a recruitment agency in the Philippines, which resulted in interviews and a short written exam. Just getting this interview requires teacher credentials and several years teaching experience in a high-demand area (math, science, and special education).
- The second rung: Those deemed worthy to move up the ladder were then invited to a large hotel ballroom meeting for the next round of screening—at which they found themselves with five hundred plus teachers taking, in the case of California, the mini-California Basic Educational Skills Test (CBEST).[9] They

were then given a break and asked to reconvene some hours later. When they gathered again, the agency read out the names of about a hundred teachers and excused the rest.

- The third rung: The teachers who were chosen participated in the coveted interview with the American school district personnel. Of the original 500 who walked into the ballroom at the start of the process, fifty might walk out with the prized precontract for an American teaching position.
- The last two steps: The fifty teachers who made it to the top of the ladder felt like they had won the lottery. Of course, they couldn't hop into the transnational labor market chute until they had raised more than three times their annual salary to pay for the prize. Making this last step was generally a move into debt with a high-stakes payoff.

Labor theorists often compare the degree to which an occupation is gated—the difficulty in passing through the professional gateway, so to speak—with the degree of respect given the occupation. Teaching has been historically characterized by ease of entry[10] and some reform efforts to improve the quality of teachers have concentrated on increasing the entry standards—higher education, more time, greater expense. It is certainly the case that the Filipino teachers who make it to the United States feel like they are among the most elite of teachers. In fact, U.S. teaching experience is a mark of status for returning Filipino teachers. A high-paying teaching position in the United States is evidence that the teacher has what it takes to earn such a reward. This feeling of being among the select few seems to heighten the stakes—to make it all the more important that the teacher succeed. An early return is a failure and a fall from elite status back home.

Pathway Implications

The various pathways seem correlated with supply. Individual pathways bring very few teachers, government-sponsored pathways bring more, and the market mechanisms of recruitment agencies bring the vast bulk of overseas trained teachers. It seems that the increasing numbers of OTTs in the United States have been facilitated by recruitment agencies. These agencies sit outside the normal organizational context of schooling and teachers' work and are, by and large, unregulated by the educational system. Second, pathways influence teacher expectations and experience of work in the United States. The teachers from Spain find their government pathway here easy and relatively inexpensive and they are ready to make the return journey if conditions don't suit them. The Filipinos find their agency pathway steep, arduous, and expensive. They do not readily return home and their relative success here is imbued with a much greater significance in their lives. Of course, it isn't easy to explicate the pathway story from the motivations. Teacher motivation, coupled with institutional pathways, influences how teachers orient to and navigate their experience.

Chutes and Ladders

An interesting labor market dynamic is confronting migrating teachers. For the largest share of teachers—those coming from developing countries who are motivated by an economic desire to move from poverty— the experience resembles a game of chutes and ladders. Teachers in developing countries must make their way to the top of their home nation's career ladders in order to get into a chute that takes them to the bottom of the industrialized country's teacher labor market. This obviously alters the traditional local and national boundaries of teacher labor markets, but it also creates new motivations to teach—essentially replacing intrinsic motivations to teach with the new extrinsic motivations to migrate.

Moving Up and Sliding Down

This chutes and ladders phenomenon is clearly experienced by the Filipino teachers in their movement to California schools. That process of moving up the selection ladder—from initial screening to the exam in the hotel ballroom with hundreds of others, to the special selected few who make it to the interview stage, on to the elite who actually land a teaching contract with an industrialized country—is a very tangible example of the labor market ladder that these teachers must climb in order to take the express ride to the schools that are hardest-to-staff in the United States. In the Philippines, selection for transnational migration positions the teachers as high status. In the United States, being identified as transnational positions teachers as low status employees who need to accept posts in schools that others think of as "hell."

The same is true in New Zealand. In 2008, half of the applicants for vacant teaching posts in New Zealand were educated in other countries. While the country of origin of these teachers seeking employment in New Zealand is not reported, what is evident is that they are considered less desirable than domestically educated teachers. As one school principal reported in a New Zealand newspaper article on the topic, he would not hire overseas trained teachers for his school as he does not deem them as capable and effective as native teachers. He warns, though, that " eventually, somebody is going to employ them . . . Down the food chain there may be some schools that will just take whoever's left and put them in front of kids and then it is very difficult."[11]

This pattern is also evidenced in the South Africa to England teacher migration pathway. As in the United States, the overseas trained teachers in England are mainly concentrated in high-poverty schools. For example, in 2005, only 7 percent of teachers in outer London schools were overseas trained, while 13 percent of teachers in inner London schools were overseas trained. Furthermore that 13 percent jumped to 20 percent in just the high-poverty London borough of Hackney. Where poverty is concentrated, so too are low-status OTTs concentrated.[12]

This fits with the reasons English head teachers gave for hiring OTTs. In a survey of 340 head teachers, McNamara, Lewis, and Howson (2007) found that 70 percent hired OTTs only when they were unable to recruit UK trained teachers.[13] This underlines the point, borne out also in the interviews with American school administrators, that schools seek to hire internationally only when they are unable to hire domestically.

When industrialized countries do hire overseas, they are able to pull from the "top tier" of developing nations, creating teacher shortages that might not be readily perceivable. Appleton and colleagues (2006) refer to this as the "ripple effect."[14] For example, formerly white and affluent South African schools are the most frequently tapped sources for teachers recruited to English schools. Schools that had previously served students racially categorized as "colored" or Indian are the next most frequently tapped. While top-tier schools that lose teachers directly to the international market reported ease in filling those posts, mid- and lower-tier schools have difficulty filling teaching posts, especially in high-need areas like math and science. The formerly white schools have an abundance of teacher supply while other schools report challenges in refilling posts—in part because they lose teachers both to the international market and to the formerly white schools.

This pattern of teacher recruitment and distribution is played out within England as well. The higher status schools in England employ domestic teachers, while the lower status English schools employ the higher status South African teachers. The lower status South African schools seek teachers further down their own domestic social and economic hierarchy. This unquestionably affects the supply and distribution of teachers globally from a purely distributional perspective; but, just as importantly, it influences teachers' motivations to teach, with the lure of economic migration sometimes taking the place of more intrinsically motivated goals.[15]

As the next chapter details, more than three quarters of the Filipino teachers studied entered special eduction in order to migrate for the extrinsic reward of higher income. Notably, the South African to England migration research also indicates that teacher motivation is shifted from the intrinsic rewards of student success, community development, and professional contribution to the extrinsic rewards of salary—sometimes at the cost of student learning.

At the end of an account of South African teacher migration to England in search of greener pastures, Manik (2007) shares the experience of South African teachers who felt frustrated by English student discipline problems and the associated feelings of teacher dissatisfaction and ineffectiveness. Some returned home rather than continue on without success—but others opted to accept the student disrespect and misbehavior and to lower their expectations of students in order to achieve their financial goals as teachers.

A South African overseas teacher named Charlie says he knows how to cope with the disappointments he has encountered in England: "You turn, put your hands in your pockets and think pounds."[16] In effect, Charlie's caring about students is replaced by a caring for the income teaching can generate—just as Alma Cruz's insistence on student attention and learning is replaced by her goal of supporting her family and facilitating their reunion through immigration. These are unnecessary dichotomies. Teachers can care about both their students and their professional income. They shouldn't have to choose between setting high standards for student achievement and being reunited with their families.

In Sum

The extrinsic motivation of increased income through migration does not need to preclude the satisfaction of a job well done. Many other occupations provide both—in fact, a feature of much work thought of as "professional" is that it provides both extrinsic and intrinsic rewards. Economic motivations do not make bad teachers and are not the problem. Teachers can care about both student learning and their own remuneration. There is something going on, however, in these migrations that is forcing Alma Cruz, and teachers like her, to have to choose between doing what she knows is best as a teacher who wants to help her students, and doing what is best as a woman who is supporting her family.

The current framing of OTTs in schools forces teachers to choose, unnecessarily, between these two goals. As the next two chapters demonstrate, Alma Cruz is one of the hardest working of the OTTs. She is among the teachers who aspire to do well by her students and in her new school. She seeks to migrate successfully, to stay, and to be the highly qualified teacher sought by the United States in overseas teacher recruitment. She works, however, in a school that frames her as a short-term, transient labor option. This does not have to be the case. Schools can frame the work of overseas trained teachers in such a way that both the extrinsic and intrinsic rewards of teaching are supported.

4

There are two distinct areas of migration that teachers navigate: the point of professional entry and the manner in which teachers handle the short-term nature of the visas and, consequently, the work.

Initiating migration is often as simple as discovering a demand for your teaching expertise and going through the application process to acceptance. Sometimes, though, it means changing careers into teaching or retraining into a new teaching specialization in order to position one-self for migration.

In addition, teachers must decide how to orient themselves to the short-term limits of their visas. Some embrace the time limit, as it fits with their own goals. Others resist the limits and look for ways to extend their visas when their hope is to stay long-term. Some adapt by finding ways to work with the time limits—either making a short time teaching in America a career step, or building a career that works with a cyclical movement in and out of home and abroad as visas allow.

Teachers hoping for the long term invest much more heavily in their work, and yet have the most tenuous position in migration. Their desire to stay makes them vulnerable to exploitative employment practices. They work long hours and accept very poor working conditions in hopes of earning employer-level support for a longer-term visa, but such visas rarely materialize.

Positioning for Migration

For most teachers, the decision to migrate begins with an advertise-ment or a conversation with a friend. They learn of the opportunity, discover that they fit the type of teacher sought, find the idea appealing, and move forward to apply. This can affect the supply of teachers in sending countries and is the concern most often cited in reports on the teacher brain drain. There is a sense that industrialized countries draw the best and most experienced high-need teachers—like math and science teachers—from developing countries. There is truth to this concern; however, the lure of increased earning opportunities abroad is not just drawing teachers to teach in America—it is drawing some people into the teaching profession itself. The economics of transnational migration is altering the career contours and profile of the teaching profession.

Teaching for Migration

Some enter teaching or change their subject area in order to migrate. Renata Romero worked most of her career in banking, but a desire to migrate out of the Philippines led her to retrain as a special education teacher. A mother of three, she says that she "saw the writing on the wall." Her reasoning was straightforward: "Looking at the trend of things happening in my country, I knew it was going to get worse [economically]." In order to provide a decent future for her children, she decided that she had to emigrate elsewhere. She considered careers that would improve her chances for permanent migration. She considered nursing but decided special education was more of a growing field. After twenty years in banking, she returned to school and studied special education, earning a master's degree in the field. The hardest part, she said, was getting her necessary teaching experience to qualify for the U.S. market. Her home city was flooded with people retraining for special education—many of them sharing her intent to migrate. In the end, she paid the Filipino school where she did her student teaching internship to let her teach there. One year after completing her master's in education, a year during which she paid for work experience, she applied for and was hired as a California-based special education teacher on an H1B visa. During the following two years, she managed to bring her children over, and she has changed employers to a school district known to sponsor teachers' green card applications. She is focused and determined to migrate permanently.

Although Renata is exceptionally determined and savvy in seeking out the optimal employment routes to permanent U.S. residency, her story is highly typical in that she entered special education in order to migrate. Teachers in the Philippines are retraining as special education teachers, or entering teaching as special education teachers, in order to teach in the United States. Fifteen of the nineteen Filipino special education teachers interviewed in California had become special education teachers for the express purpose of migrating abroad. The labor market needs of the United States affected their career goals, teaching orientations, and personal lives. The possible economic gain of teaching overseas was a major draw into special education. Teaching, and specifically teaching special education overseas, provided a very clear career trajectory that offered economic upward mobility.

Leveraging Experience to Migrate

In contrast, the Filipino science and math teachers interviewed shared the economic motivations of the special education teachers, but none of them were recent entries to the field. All had many years teaching in their subject areas. They did not enter teaching in order to migrate, but migrate they did when the opportunity presented itself. In fact, there was a general sense that the better teachers were the ones who could migrate— that migration itself was a distinguishing feature of teacher quality. Nina Flores, a fifty-nine-year-old math teacher who entered the United States eight years ago after twenty-two years of teaching at an elite private school in the Philippines, contends that all the private school math teachers have been leaving their Filipino teaching posts to seek work in the United States. Nina has an H1B visa and her green card is pending. Provided she gets her permanent residency, she plans to work until she retires at sixty-six. Meanwhile, Maria Reyes, a thirty-five-year-old chemistry teacher with fifteen years of teaching experience in the Philippines, is working under her second three-year cultural exchange visa. It is unclear whether she will be granted another new visa, but she comforts herself with the knowledge that her time in the United States will have increased her marketability back home. She explains the situation this way: "There is a prestige [from teaching in the United States]. If you went back to the Philippines and then people there, especially at the schools, are aware that you are a teacher in America, you are really proud of it."

None of the math and science teachers interviewed had fewer than four years of teaching experience in their field prior to migrating—and actually, only three of them had fewer than ten years. Most of the math and science teachers had advanced degrees in their field and many years of teaching experience. All of them reported migrating for economic gain, but none of them entered their field to migrate. It may be that the costs of entry—in terms of both time and money—are just too great in science and math to merit a career change to facilitate migration. Special education credentials can be gained through one year of graduate study in the Philippines, regardless of the undergraduate major, but math and science require subject matter expertise. Perhaps, over time, more Filipinos will seek math and science teaching credentials in order to migrate to the United States—yet this remains to be seen.

Orienting to Short-Term Migration

The overseas trained teachers all arrive on short-term visas, but the way they view those visas places them in two categories that affect their engagement with the work and their migration experience. The first are the embracers—teachers who embrace the short-term nature of the visas and tend to invest the least in their students and schools. The second are the aspirers—those who aspire to stay in their U.S.-based teaching posts and invest the greatest amount of time and energy into their schools, students, and careers—even when there is no rational hope that they will achieve permanent status.

Embracers

The global adventurers of Spain represent the embracers—teachers who embrace the short-term nature of the work and seek ways to maximize their pleasure in the time they have. They forgo studying for teaching exams, preferring instead to spend their time pursuing leisure activities. Failing the exams may require an early return to Spain, but passing up travel opportunities for exam preparation runs contrary to their own short-term orientation. For the most part, they do not intend to stay in the United States, as one teacher from Spain explained: "I live near the beach even though the rent is higher and the drive to work longer. While I am here on holiday—um, I mean, working—I want to be in a nice place."

Her use of the term "holiday"—though quickly corrected—reveals the general orientation shared by the teachers from Spain interviewed. Their regular social gatherings are peppered with conversation about recent weekend trips, shared tips on best airline deals to popular U.S. destinations, and debates on whether it is best to drive or fly to the Grand Canyon. It is not that they do not work hard—they do. But, as Alejandro says, they want to teach and do other things. Investing energy in required credentials to stay long-term does not seem necessary when one has no intention to stay long-term. They are on a "working holiday" that involves both the work and the holiday aspects of the experience.

Aspirers

The aspirers—the economically motivated teachers—approach the short-term visa differently. They imagine that if they can distinguish themselves through hard work and perseverance, that they can be among the few to merit and gain employer sponsorship for permanent status.

Faith Torrez is an example. Faith taught science for ten years in the Philippines and arrived in 2006 on a J-1 visa. She has worked hard for three years as a science teacher in an urban high school, spending weekends studying for her teaching exams, prepping for her classes, and attending additional professional development courses to help her succeed with her new students. She has passed her California state teaching exams, developed relationships with her students, and earned positive evaluations from her school principal. She even went through the arduous and expensive process of getting the Philippines to waive the two-year repatriation clause in the J-1 visa. Nevertheless, the district sponsorship of her H1B visa is not likely. She never participated in the state-mandated new teacher induction programs required for a clear state teaching credential. She did not understand that was a requirement and, according to Faith, no one ever told her it was expected or offered her the support to participate in the programs. As she faces the end of her three-year cultural exchange visa, she hopes the district will sponsor her for the H1B labor shortage visa, but she has come to see that her sponsorship is unlikely:

> I love this school. If I will be given the chance, to choose, to stay, then okay! If the principal would say, "We are going to fight for you to stay here." Then yes! I love this school. I love the kids. I'm just not ready [to leave]. But umm, here's the thing, if they are going to send me back, send us back home, they are going to find other teachers to replace us.*

*Faith Torres is talking about both herself and about overseas trained teachers in general. She has come to understand that the school sees both her and her follow OTTs as readily replaceable. Her reference here to "us" is a reference to all OTTS.

70

Faith is not unusual. Of the thirty-three Filipino teachers interviewed, thirty of them aspire to turn their J-1 three-year visas into six-year H1Bs, and then perhaps into permanent residency. They hope for this even though they are unable to name a single teacher they know who has successfully navigated this process. They are like high school basketball players with NBA hopes. Even if they know the odds are not in their favor, they hope they will be the one exception. They talk of being "tough," working hard, and beating the odds.

And the odds are not in their favor. A school district official where Faith teaches explained the situation clearly:

> It's almost impossible to do [to move from a J-1 to an H1B visa], but I know of several (Filipino teachers) that are trying to do it . . . but it's a gamble.
>
> They have to pass all their tests, not only CBEST but CSET, which is much harder. They have to pass all their tests and they have to do BTSA . . . They have to have a good recommendation from their principal and a statement that their principal will take them back. Then, before they can apply for their H1B, they go back and do the thing that they do in the Philippines and get the waiver . . . then if they get the H1B, they can come back on the H1B in October. So far we have had no one, and I say, we've had no one who has done it. To my knowledge, there's no one.

This district official emphasizes that the challenges are particularly hard for special education teachers. Due to the time limits of their J-1 visas, they need to complete the credential requirements in three years that new American special education teachers have five years to complete. Despite these seemingly insurmountable odds, sixteen of the nineteen special education teachers interviewed hoped that they would manage to overcome the obstacles and permanently migrate.

This alters the way they engage with the work and their personal situations. Rather than pay a higher rent to live by the beach, they live in close quarters with many other teachers to minimize housing costs and maximize their savings. Instead of spending weekends traveling, they spend them studying for teacher exams, taking graduate classes, grading students' papers, and prepping lesson plans. Many of these Filipino teachers see permanent immigration as the way to secure their financial stability. This is, in many ways, an inaccurate perception.

Diminishing Returns: A Cautionary Tale

Impressed by teacher salaries in U.S. schools, many Filipinos set permanent visas and the relocation of their families to the United States as a goal. Those who achieve this goal quickly realize that their financial advantage is lost when salary and the expenses of supporting a family are in the same geographic and financial location. This consolidation of their professional and personal lives confronts them with the financial challenges of supporting a family on teachers' wages.

Most of the Filipino teachers expressed the desire to migrate permanently, bring their families, and settle in the United States. Few of them know Lailani Razon and her cautionary tale. A math teacher with twenty years of teaching experience, she left her teaching position at a Manila private school for a public school teaching post in California. She navigated the visa process, from the J-1 cultural exchange visa she entered on in 2002 to the waived repatriation clause, and in 2005 she obtained an H1B labor shortage visa. Like other teachers from the Philippines, she experienced a dramatic leap in pay when she moved from Manila to California—in her first month teaching in the United States, she earned more than her annual salary in the Philippines—and this increase afforded significant changes in her family living conditions. Her sons, still in the Philippines, received an elite private education there and her whole family lived very well on her salary. Her migration didn't just make them comfortable—it made them affluent. Her children went to school with some of the wealthiest families in Manila. Her family enjoyed an unprecedented standard of living—both for themselves and for the family of a teacher.

Things have changed since she brought her family to live in California with her. Her teacher salary does not afford a lavish lifestyle in the United States—especially not in the metropolitan areas where overseas teachers are concentrated. Once her sons joined her here, they attended urban public schools. They recently reached college age and the family found themselves unable to afford college. Her children do not qualify for financial aid—and won't until they are all at least permanent residents. As a foreign national on a temporary labor shortage visa, she sits outside of the normal support structures. Her teacher migration only helped her children's educational prospects while they stayed behind in the Philippines. Although Lailani managed to buy a small house here, she is finding it difficult to afford the mortgage payments, which require most of her income. Her financial advantage was thus lost through family reunification in the United States.

How the Adaptors Make the Process Work

Other OTTs become adaptors who accept their short-term visa status and find ways to make it work for them as a career step or career model. Some of the savviest Filipino migrant teachers are well aware of this conundrum. The teachers who are more cosmopolitan—those who have come from the main cities, traveled previously, and have networked global connections—tend to know that financial success is possible as long as they earn in the United States and spend in the Philippines. These advantages are lost once the family finds itself living in the same economy in which the teacher works. Consequently, many OTTs do not aim for immigration. They make three- to six-year stints in the United States part of a larger development plan. Three teachers interviewed explained their intent to leverage their temporary U.S. stay into a schooling business in the Philippines—specifically, the founding of private schools. Three years in the United States would provide the funds for the school and the U.S. teaching experience would provide them increased status at home. If possible, they also hope to earn a U.S. graduate degree as an added boon to their status and ability to draw students.

Nimuel Ramirez, who once considered washing dishes in the United States to pay his sister's medical costs, has set his sights on earning the funds needed to open a private school in the Philippines.[1] He does not want to relocate his wife and daughter to the United States—nor does he want to return to the small pay scale of a teacher in the Philippines. Opening his own school is something he feels his U.S. salary will allow him to afford:

> As I grow older, I haven't seen myself, whether in teaching or another profession, being financially stable and secure. So I have thought of maybe finding an alternative way. I have a dream of putting up my own school someday. I have directed schools before. I can put up my own school and this will be a great opportunity for me to financially gain from it . . . in teaching in the United States so I can earn the money to open the school . . . I decided to set a goal of opening my own private school back home.

Karen del Mundo has a similar goal. For several years before leaving the Philippines to teach in the United States, Karen owned and ran a small reading center for students with learning disabilities. Her decision to teach in the United States was part of an intentional strategy to increase the size and status of her center. Three years in the United States was all she needed to earn an American graduate degree, gain U.S. work experience, and earn enough income to expand the school and garner it new attention. Her sister kept things going in her absence and the two of them worked together to implement their development plan.

> My goal is to save money, earn a master's in reading, and get U.S. teaching experience . . . I have this small reading center that I opened [back home] . . . and I left it with my sister and then another teacher. They are managing it right now . . . And then we plan on building it up when I get home. I don't have intentions of extending [my] J1 visa, so I hope to get everything done in the three-year time that I am here . . . and then build up my center.

Karen's decision to attend graduate school in the United States reflects the connection between the motivation of increased status and the motivation of improved economics. The latter is in service to the former. "Back in the Philippines, if you have a degree from somewhere else—from somewhere overseas—it's like a big deal. It's like you are more qualified than if you just had one from back home."

Increased status is gained through a U.S.-based university education, but the American teaching experience alone appears to imbue the teacher returning to the Philippines with increased status. Clara Suarez, a teacher with sixteen years of teaching experience in the Philippines, certainly had that in mind when she chose the name for her future school, the International School for Special Children: "I was thinking, I wanted it [to be] 'international' because, you see, they [future students and their parents] would know that I came from America and then they would be impressed."

Clara does not intend to bring her children to the United States, because she realizes she can afford a better education for them in the Philippines. Her preference is to stay in the United States throughout the remainder of her children's secondary and university education in the Philippines—about ten years. Her J-1 visa, however, only permits a three-year stay with a mandatory repatriation clause of two years. Her solution is to open a private special education center with other overseas teachers, an option that will allow them to cycle in and out of U.S. public school teaching and Philippines-based private teaching. The demand for special education teachers led her to shift, after sixteen years, from values education to special education.[2] Now, the visa and economic realities of teacher migration are giving shape to new transnational career plans.

Oh, after this I'd like to build a small center, just a small center for special ed . . . special ed center back home. Me and my friends are teachers, we're like planning, you'd be the director, you'd be like the . . . I'll be the overseeing officer, something like that, and then okay. You start out . . . I'll go home and start out this project. I'll start out this center and then I will go back to the United States and work still and then go back, just go back and forth from the Philippines and the United States and overseas. That would be my dream.

In this way, Clara imagines that they can share profits and responsibilities—a transnational teacher profit co-op, if you will. Karen is supporting her sister, who is keeping shop back home. Rather than fight repatriation, Clara and her friends hope to open a private school that assumes a percentage of its teacher workforce is always in the United States—and that those teachers will tag team with the home-based teachers to keep both the Philippines-based school going and the U.S. income stream viable. It is a model that assumes and requires a transnational labor market economy.

All three of these savvy Filipino teachers have figured out a way to make a short-term teaching stay in the United States part of their larger career goals in order to adapt to limited economic opportunities back home. Recognizing both the barriers to, and the limits of, more permanent migration, they have identified teaching in the United States as a stepping-stone to their goals rather than as the end goal. The turnover of OTTs seems inevitable to them. Karen and Nimuel will use their three years to position themselves to open schools upon repatriation. Clara and her friends have devised a plan that allows for cycling in and out of America as shuttlecocks in a global badminton game.

Teacher migration opportunities have changed the direction of their careers, and the focus of their teaching. For example, all three of them are special education teachers, but only Karen has any long-term involvement with the field. Nimuel and Clara shifted from other teaching areas to special education in order to fit the U.S. labor market demands. Their orientation to teaching was affected by their motivations to improve their economic situation.

The current reality is that while some Filipinos are being drawn into special education teaching for migration purposes, all Filipino teachers are motivated to migrate for economic reasons. Some teachers plan to maximize these economic gains in short-term placements for long-term plans back home, others hope to extend their stays to achieve longer-term goals, while still others seek to emigrate to the United States permanently. The prestige of having taught in the United States is an added boon to many, at the same time, marking them as qualified teachers back home and conferring on them a prestige they can leverage for new career opportunities. Getting, and keeping, their U.S. teaching positions is an important career move for the economically motivated teachers from the Philippines.

Empowerment and Exploitation

Teachers motivated by global adventure are in a position of power when it comes to school site placement, teaching assignments, and working conditions. Unlike their economically motivated counterparts, they will not migrate without their families, they do not accept positions at schools they judge to offer poor working conditions and supports, and they will complain about their treatment and work context to school administrators. They see an early return to their home country as a viable option if the work proves unsuitable or unpleasant. This affects the way they engage with students, colleagues, and administrators.

The most interesting aspect of the global adventurers is the contrast they offer to the economic improvement seekers. Global adventurers have typically embraced the short-term nature of their visas and fully intend to return to their home countries. Most economic improvement seekers, however, are aspiring to extend their visas, ideally indefinitely or at least to leverage it into the next career move. This creates an interesting set of contrasts and constraints.

The economically motivated tend to invest more time and money into their own professional development in an effort to become more desirable employees. They spend their weekends preparing for state teacher exams, while the global adventurers spend their weekends exploring locally and traveling more widely. The latter are unwilling to invest too heavily in a short-term placement. The latter, however, also have more bargaining power in placements and working conditions, essentially because they have options.

Economics as a motivation leads many to a dual experience of empowerment and exploitation. They are empowered by a massive shift in earning ability—and they are also easily exploited by the urgent need to retain their U.S. teaching positions to sustain that advantage. A move from the Philippines to the United States allows teachers to increase annual earnings from about $3,000 to $60,000-plus U.S. dollars. Acquiring the U.S. teaching position, however, generally requires teachers to initially both borrow heavily at high interests rates to pay placement fees and to leave their families behind—a condition of the visa sponsor.

Retaining a highly paid U.S. teaching position and getting visa sponsor permission for family reunification requires a positive evaluation by administrators at the school where teachers work. These evaluations reportedly require teacher loyalty to the administration and acceptance of unpleasant working conditions. Economically motivated OTTs generally avoid labor action, for example, as the risk is too high. They rarely complain about working conditions and they accept any teaching post offered no matter how challenging the work environment.

They repeatedly hear the same messages: (1) function autonomously and don't be a bother to your school principal, (2) maintain classroom order as it is not okay to have discipline problems, and (3) be accommodating to your colleagues and administrators. As one school district official told a roomful of newly arrived Filipino OTTs: "You don't ever send a student out of the room unless they physically threaten you. Your principal needs to know you can handle the students on your own."

This leads some of the teachers to limit their expectations of students rather than push for performance—trading pedagogical practice and high expectations for student behavioral compliance. The costs are too high to do anything but comply. The potential loss of the high-paying position, the debt incurred, and the desire to be reunited with family leave them vulnerable to exploitation. This pits teachers' goals for income and migration against their goals for student achievement and well-being.

Consider Rodel Bautista, for example, currently the sole overseas trained teacher at his school. Arriving in 2007 with 100 other Filipino teachers recruited by a single urban Californian school district, he and nine of his "batch mates" were hired into the same high-poverty, high teacher-turnover school, a school with a reputation for being the "toughest" in the district and filled with students "not ready to learn." According to Rodel, most American teachers leave the school. "Some of the teachers remain—but most teachers in the school leave after their first year of teaching." His Filipino batch mates left too, but not by choice. They were not renewed after receiving poor principal evaluations due to weak classroom management skills. Yet, they also received no support from the school to make the transition to their new students, classrooms, school, and culture. Rodel himself, the only one of the ten whose contract was renewed for a second year, was not expected to make it. His principal told him during his end-of-year-one evaluation that she was surprised he had made it. According to him, she said, "I never knew that you would be good. I'm sorry. I thought you would be not making it even to the end of this [first] year."

New to special education. Rodel concedes that it was challenging. He taught music and general education for six years in the Philippines prior to earning his special education degree. Like many of his batch mates, he sought the special education degree as his passport to the United States and higher income opportunities. He saw taking the U.S. job as a gamble that could either greatly advantage or significantly hurt his family. He funded the placement fees by selling his land, car, furniture, and—as he shared with tears in his eyes—his pride. Humbled, he sold his possessions, borrowed heavily at high interest rates, moved his wife and children in with extended family, left his teaching post at the school he himself attended and his children currently attend, and accepted a position, sight unseen, in a school situated far away. He felt he had no other choice:"Here's the opportunity. I'll grab it. I had no other choice. If I don't go with this choice, I might not get a school. I might not get my salary." In the Philippines, he made $2,000 a year. In the United States, his salary jumped to $60,000 annually. But to win this gamble, he had to meet the requirements for keeping his job.

He talks about the massive adjustments he had to make to teach special education in a new place and culture:

> The most challenging would be the first month. Considering that on my part we prepared the IEPs, the reports for each child, individualized lessons for each of the kids. That was hard for me because we didn't have enough training to understand that system and how it works. We had a system in the Philippines which is completely different from here. And second thing is, uh, one of my greatest challenges was when—when kids are speaking, they talk too fast, eh, including adults. They don't speak like us that—it's

like we're kind of slow in teaching in saying the language, but we always make sure it's said properly, and I know that's okay and sometimes we have to go through what they meant . . . to better understand if we had that communication and—uh we understood each other and that is one of the hindrances.

Challenges . . . challenges . . . oh the culture. Definitely the culture. On the physical aspect and everything. Well, my students are taller than I. And it's so hard to, uh . . . uh well, my principal was teasing me that, "Your students are even taller than you." And she had second thoughts of getting me back then because I was short.

Without mentorship, with only a week's generic orientation and an administrator who hired him while anticipating his failure, Rodel had to deduce the form and function of individual education plans (IEPs, in special education speak), stumble through attempts to run IEP meetings with parents, and put together active outings and community activities with pedagogical merit for his students. He achieved the first by reading through student files and writing new IEPs modeled on the students' former ones. He developed skills at running meetings through trial and error. "You learn," he remarks ruefully, "to give them the positive things about their child before you tell them about the negative, and then you have a better meeting result." And by asking other teachers many questions—as he says, by "not being ashamed to ask questions." Working long hours and being organized, he managed to find the resources he needed to plan engaging lesson outings for students to the barbershop, car wash, and other businesses and community centers. He learned to make school fun for his students and to thereby manage his classrooms and students without the disruptions that could cost him his job and make him a loser in his financial gamble.

Rodel Bautista and his batch mates experienced a high-stakes case of 'sink or swim'—one that threw them in the deep end with few resources and the full expectation that they were unlikely to make it. Classroom management problems would, and did, cost most of them their jobs. Rodel gambled and won; the other nine gambled and lost. They borrowed heavily, sold possessions, changed their family circumstances—and went home in debt, without work waiting for them and to families that depended on them for support. Stories of these teachers and the risk of this failure have an allegorical quality to them among the other

Filipino teachers. The importance of classroom management—controlling students to the satisfaction of the school administrators—is repeated continually, shared by the established and successful second- and third-year teachers with the newly arrived. It is embraced by one and all as a mantra:

Good classroom management means renewal.
Poor classroom management means failure and dismissal.
Please your principal and keep your job.

The increased salary opportunity does empower economically motivated teachers to better support their families—but, coupled with the conditions of tenuous work security and the vulnerability of debt, the limited alternatives expose them to the real possibility, and often reality, of exploitation. Teachers accept long working hours and take on any additional task asked of them, although working in a job with no long-term security. They may have a contract and a credential. They may even earn tenure—but their visa can be revoked at any time, making the rest irrelevant. Teachers with revoked visas are left to bear the costs of travel home with no recourse to the American safety net of unemployment. The agency that brought them here has little investment in their success. In fact, the agencies make the bulk of their profit through placement fees. One teacher's failure is the potential for additional income in the form of another teacher's placement fee to the agency.

In Sum

In many ways, this is an age-old American story of the immigrant dream. Great sacrifice, endured in the interest of possible future gain, comes with trials and tribulations acting as a sorting mechanism. Not everyone can get to the so-called Promised Land. Only the best and brightest will prevail—and so on. But this isn't just a story about immigrant dreams. These immigrants are not the miners and field workers of historical migrations, nor are they the engineers and nurses of newer migrations. They are the teachers of some of the most needy students in the United States. How are the overseas trained teachers—given their pathways, motivations, and personal navigations—positioned as teachers in American high-poverty schools? How are they framed as teachers there? How do they engage with the work and what are the consequences for American students and society?

The next chapter looks at the tale of two schools and how most schools frame OTTs as transients, high-turnover schools that presume and cultivate short-term teachers. Teachers migrating to something— like global adventure—can and do avoid these transient schools. Teachers migrating from things like economic deprivation are more likely to take what they can get. Some schools, however, can and do frame teachers as transplants, and these are schools that seek to retain and develop the teachers they recruit. The school-level framing of overseas teachers has consequences for how teachers engage with students and is an essential element in determining the relative success of overseas trained teachers.

5

A TALE OF TWO SCHOOLS

The Transient School and the Transplant School

There are best-case and worst-case scenarios for overseas trained teachers working in U.S. public schools. There are schools that frame overseas teachers as transplants—valuable resources that must be nurtured through the relocation process to ensure that they take root and flourish. And there are schools that frame overseas teachers as transients—temporarily needed resources that are passing through and readily replaceable.

Whether OTTs end up at a transplant school or a transient school has significant implications for their experience, adjustment, and success. In fact, it is a critical piece in determining an OTT's experience and effectiveness. Yet, not all teachers are equally well positioned to know this or to be selective in their decision making. The least empowered are the most likely to end up in the most difficult situations—and the implications for students are disturbing.

Teachers migrating to something—global adventure, climate, professional opportunity—are well positioned to be selective in their school choice. They are willing to forgo the experience if they are unable to find a work placement that fits their requirements. They have nothing, or at least little, to lose if the U.S. experience is not successful. On the other hand, teachers migrating from something—especially economic deprivation—have a great deal to lose. They need their U.S. positions to escape economic challenges and they want to stay. This latter group of teachers is less well positioned to be selective in their workplace choices—even though the stakes are higher for them. Their diminished agency, in fact, stems from the higher stakes that they face. Teachers migrating from economic deprivation are more likely to end up at schools that frame them as transients—thereby creating a double set of barriers to their hopes for success.

82

Transient schools frame OTTs as short-term labor solutions. A parallel framing would be the migrant or guest worker, for example, hired to pick seasonal crops then sent home. Transient schools hire OTTs because they are unable to recruit domestic teachers, but also because they accept high staffing turnover as a given. The churn of faculty and administration in these schools is the norm, an accepted condition of work for all faculty—not just those who are trained overseas. Consequently, these schools do little to retain teachers. The support mechanisms administrators might put into place to retain teachers become an unnecessary expense if high turnover is expected and accepted.

Do transient schools embrace a short-term labor model because of high turnover—or does high turnover result from a school-level transient orientation to the teacher labor market? In either case, OTTs at transient schools find it far more difficult to successfully transition to U.S. classroom teaching than teachers at more transplant-oriented schools.

Transplant schools frame OTTs as resources to be developed and retained. These are schools where the transnational teachers sought are intended to transition into permanent roles within the school and the community. Schools that seek to transplant teachers from another country are also schools that frame their overall teacher workforce as stable and retainable. School leaders in such schools expect teachers to stay, and therefore they support teachers—inducting them into the profession, the school, and the community, and empowering them to shape the school even as the school shapes them. Overseas trained teachers who land at transplant schools appear to be far more successful at transitioning to successful U.S. classroom teaching, meaning that they are more likely to succeed beyond the first year, to achieve results with students, and to immigrate permanently as teachers in the United States.

Both transient and transplant schools affect the composition of the U.S. teacher workforce. Transplant schools grow the overall U.S. teacher workforce, expanding its ranks. Transient schools increase the U.S. reliance on a high-turnover teacher workforce, extending the revolving door's entry point outside its national borders. Of course, the successful transition of OTTs into the United States is a result of many interacting factors. Two clearly indicated ones, however, are teacher position within the workforce and school orientation to the teacher workforce.

As evidenced in Chapters 3 and 4, teacher position is influenced by motivation to migrate. Teachers migrating from hardships such as economic disadvantage are less likely to succeed than teachers migrating to something like travel and professional opportunities. This is, in large part, because the former are less likely to find work in transplant schools. Their desperation to secure a position, born out of a lack of viable alternatives at home, leads them to accept teaching posts based on little information and reflection. Their intent is to secure employment, and they often find themselves in what Liu and Moore-Johnson have termed an "information poor" hiring process—one that gives schools and teachers alike little information about one another beyond the basic teaching credentials.[1] Information poor hiring is done far from the classroom and late in the process. Schools that invest in an "information rich" hiring process practice decentralized decision making, have teachers interview with school personnel closest to the teachers' working lives (i.e., department heads and colleagues rather than principals and district personnel), and hire teachers well before the start of the school year.

Transient schools offer posts more readily than transplant schools—and with far less of an information rich hiring process. Teachers who feel least resourced are the most likely to accept hastily offered and barely previewed teaching positions. The desperate schools find the desperate teachers, compounding the problems for both. There is evidence, however, that a transplant school can facilitate the adjustment and retention of even a teacher migrating from disadvantage. This suggests the critical importance of work context in understanding the experience of OTTs in U.S. schools.

There are implications for students as well as teachers and schools. High teacher turnover is correlated with lower student achievement, even when the schools studied are controlled for student demographics.[2] In addition, schools that utilize effective teacher induction supports are known to achieve higher results sooner with students.[3] When high turnover is combined with low supports for new teachers, the negative implications for student experience are compounded. Transient schools not only create a difficult transnational teacher experience; they also may contribute to low academic achievement for American students.

The rest of this chapter features two schools that draw heavily on the OTT labor market—especially as related to the Philippines. New Urban High School is a transient school, and Alma Cruz, the teacher featured in the introduction to this book, struggles to sustain herself there. Across town, Malaya Mundo, another Filipino OTT, thrives at Central High School, a transplant school that has made it possible for Malaya to stay as a teacher in the United States. Both schools are in the same urban school district. They are large and overcrowded, run on a year-round schedule of multiple tracks. They both serve a high-poverty, majority Latino, and large English language learner population. From the outside, they look much the same in so many ways. However, Central High School is much more successful at supporting teachers and students. Its teachers stay longer and its students achieve at higher levels. New Urban High School, in contrast, experiences high teacher turnover and lower student achievement. One school district yet two realities.

The Transient School: New Urban High School

There are twenty-four Filipino OTTs at New Urban High School, including ten of the twenty-four math teachers and eleven of the sixteen science teachers. They make up 15 percent of the school's teacher work-force. All are here on three-year visas. When asked why the school hired overseas trained teachers, vice principal Janice Burns replied, "It was either substitutes or Filipinos." Given the labor market options as she saw them, the administrators elected to acquire the subject specialism that the Filipino teachers have to offer. "Maybe the Filipino teachers will reach one or two students in the class—that is one or two more than a substitute would reach."

When Susan Krado, another school administrator, was asked what the school would do if they were unable to renew the Filipino teachers' visas, she said, "If they leave, we will just hire more [Filipino teachers]. They are motivated, don't complain, and work hard." When asked if she was concerned about the high turnover that results from such a practice, her answer was clear: "No one stays at New Urban High School—not the teachers and not the principals. I won't stay. Everyone is passing through."

New Urban High School opened in 2005, almost completely staffed with substitute and intern teachers. In the winter of 2009, the school was led by its third principal in four years. Set on the edge of a large urban downtown area, the school's modern campus is walled off from its surroundings by fencing, and it is accessed through security gates. Several buildings mark the perimeter of a central courtyard area where students eat at lunchtime but is otherwise typically vacant. All administrators carry walkie-talkies and know the difference between the code for "student with gun" versus "student with knife," and there are two fully armed police officers on campus at all times—though there have been no riots in the last year.

New Urban has four tracks of students that attend school on different academic calendars, spanning all twelve months. There are only two weeks a year that New Urban is actually closed—one week in December and one in July. Otherwise, it is a constant hive of activity serving 3,500 students in grades nine through twelve. Most of them are Latino, some of them are African American. None of them are white, nearly half are English language learners, and three-quarters of them live below the poverty level. (See Table A.1 in the appendix for school demographics.)

Staff turnover is indeed high at New Urban High School. Of the 200 adults who work in the school, only Judy Shaw—who has been in the district for thirty-four years, most of them as a teacher—has been there since it first opened four years ago. Judy was recruited to New Urban as a first-time school administrator, and almost everyone refers to her as the school's original Sentinel, referencing the school's mascot. She also functions as the school's unofficial historian, since she is the only staff member who has experienced the school's development from its inception. Many have reported that the Filipino teachers were hired because the former principal liked them, and Judy Shaw confirms this: "He [the former principal] liked them for one thing: none of the Filipino teachers caused anybody any trouble. They're very compliant and complaisant—maybe because they are afraid to complain about anything."

In 2007, there was a large staff exodus when the second principal and much of the teaching faculty left. In 2009, Judy reports that half of the teachers were in their first five years of teaching—many of them career changers enrolled in intern programs. New Urban High School has been the first teaching job for many American teachers and the first American job for many OTTs—and for many of them, their first year was their last. In an ironic example, one New Urban Filipina teacher had intended to join her sister. But, when her sister was unable to pass her state teaching exam, her sister's contract was not renewed and the school sent her back to the agency and, ultimately, to the Philippines. And, as predicted, there was another Filipina teacher ready to take her place—her newly arrived sister.

The Transplant School: Central High School

"Everyone, please take your seats," calls out tenth grade math teacher Malaya Mundo. "We have a lot to do today."

The students quickly settle in their seats, laid out in rows. There are other adults in the room, seated as a panel to one side. Made up of teachers and local community members, this panel is visiting at Ms. Mundo's request. Today is the culmination of a performance project. Students have been working in teams to plan the remodeling of a garage into a teenage boy's dream bedroom. Working from details provided about the boy's interests, the dimensions of the room, and budget restrictions, each team has developed a remodeling plan intended to maximize the room's potential. The adults on the panel are there to rate each proposal, and using a rubric provided by Ms. Mundo, and these ratings will be used to select the winning design.

Ms. Mundo runs a tight classroom. Students are eager to present their plans, and the teams move fluidly and efficiently from one to the next. The presentations, most of them using PowerPoint, highlight the floor plan, furniture selection, and cost projections. Periodically, students reference the fictitious client and his interest in computers and animation as they explain their decisions and design. The rest of the class listens attentively. The projects are varied and a general air of mutual interest and respect pervades the room.

Malaya Mundo, like Alma Cruz, is a Filipina teacher recruited to meet U.S. teacher labor needs. They teach in the same low-income school district—though in different schools. There are many ways in which the two teachers are alike and some critical ways in which they, and their experiences teaching in their school district, are markedly different. Both women have advanced degrees in mathematics and teaching experience in the Philippines. Both migrated here through an agency pathway on a J-1 cultural exchange visa for economic reasons. Both hope to continue their teaching careers in the United States. Each is positioned differently, however, both personally and professionally.

On a personal level, Malaya Mundo migrated from economic hardship; however, she had more resources to draw on and fewer demands and expenses to meet. When she migrated in 2001, teacher migration agency costs were much lower. She reports that her cost of migration was less than $2,500—still more than her annual salary in the Philippines, but nowhere near the fees—totaling three to four times their annual salaries—paid by more recent migrant teachers like Alma Cruz. Malaya Mundo was able to borrow the money from her brother, who was already living in the United States, and so did not incur the high interest rate debt nor the pressure to repay quickly. Although she has parents and siblings that she assists financially in the Philippines, she is a single woman who does not have additional pressures to support dependents or to navigate the permission process to bring them into the United States.[4]

Furthermore, Malaya teaches in a school that supports teachers as transplants, not transients. Alma Cruz is in a school that sees them as transients—nobody stays at New Urban High School, whereas the staff at Central High School works hard to support the overseas trained teachers' transition to the U.S. classroom. They want the OTTs to succeed and to stay. This is in large part a result of how the school frames teachers in general—and the overseas trained Filipino teachers in particular.

The head of the math department, Dr. Sam Fielders, describes the school and the department as a place that people want to teach, as a place that people stay. He himself has been department head for over twenty years, and many of the teachers on staff have long histories in the school and also in the community. Many of them grew up locally and several attended Central High School as students. Dr. Fielders reports having no problems recruiting teachers for his department. Although Central High School is a place where teachers want to work, he jumped at the opportunity to hire the Filipino teachers because of their outstanding quality. He has handpicked each math teacher hired over the last two decades and the Filipino teachers were a windfall. He saw them as an unexpected source of top-quality teachers whom he wanted to hire and retain. They arrived on his doorstep at exactly the right time—a series of retirements left him needing to hire a new wave of teachers. Then the school district appeared, quite literally, with a busload of Filipino teachers and handed him a stack of resumes. Going through the pile, he saw that many of them came from the top universities in the Philippines, had years of experience, and had been screened multiple times:

> When someone says they came from Berkeley and someone else went to Cal State, you know the difference. They [the Filipino teachers] went to the Berkeleys of the Philippines and they made it through with an enormous amount of training. You also have to know that these recruitment companies only took the better teachers. They don't just go and take anybody, the teachers had to go through interviews. So they have already been filtered twice for us.

Dr. Fielders was happy to hire four Filipino teachers in 2001. He has since used those teachers' contacts to hire more Filipino teachers in subsequent years. There are now nineteen Filipino OTTs at Central High

School, including ten of the school's thirty math teachers. They make up 10 percent of the school's teachers and 33 percent of its math teachers. It is a year-round school with three tracks, serving about 4,500 students—and six of the Filipino math teachers, including Ms. Mundo, teach in one track, making up 60 percent of that particular track's math teachers. While most started on three-year visas, many have already transitioned to H1B work visas, and a few even have green cards in hand.

All of the Filipino teachers hired at Central High have stayed at Central High: they have been successfully transplanted. Not that the transition was an easy one. Ms Mundo is clear that "the first year was tough," and she needed all the support she received to navigate it effectively. She arrived after the start of the school year, the language was a challenge, and the students started a countdown to when they thought she would quit. She was determined to stay the course and prove them wrong. It was challenging—the American students behaved very differently from the students she taught in the Philippines:

> Kids are very different, yes. Like in the Philippines, you will never hear a kid talk back at you. You are always, as a teacher, you are always the one who tell them what to do and there is no "but," or there is no "why like that?" But here you tell them something, "okay, let's do this class," but the student will tell you, "Why?" and you have to be ready. And for me, at first, no one told me that the students right here will really talk back at you, and argue things to you, like it's a debate for them, like that, and you have to win.

This is a common refrain with the Filipino teachers. The U.S. norms of student-teacher interactions, as well as the pedagogical practices, are very different from the norms in the Philippines. Ms. Mundo no more knew how to motivate U.S. students than the other Filipino transnational teachers—she didn't know how to navigate the school discipline and classroom management practices of the culture and the school. The difference between her and Alma Cruz is that she received the support of the other teachers and the school administrators. They taught her how to navigate the school's discipline system, encouraged her to draw on them for support, and empowered her to sustain the standards of behavior required of students:

> I didn't know that when a student misbehaves you can send them to the school office or counseling office. And then, all these [discipline]

procedures—I wasn't aware of all of those. But little by little, actually just under the first year, that's when I know, because I get support from other teachers, the teachers here are very supportive.

Cultural adjustments were needed, and those were facilitated by specific structural supports. Central High School makes it a practice to pair new OTTs with established U.S. mentor teachers. The overseas teachers both assist their mentor teachers and are supported by these established teachers in their own classrooms. Special external grant money is used to pay the OTTs to work during their intersession as supporting teachers in the classrooms of well-established American math teachers at Central High—thereby giving them further opportunity to learn from their colleagues. Teachers at Central are organized in subject-based departments and their department head—the leader most proximal to their work in terms of hiring, management and development—is knowledgeable about their subject and subject pedagogical practice. In the math department, Dr. Fielders is well-established as a leader both through his own twenty-two year tenure at the school and his advanced knowledge in the field, and he is in a good position to support the overseas math teachers' professional development.

Malaya Mundo, now in her seventh year in the United States and at the school, is working on a H1B work visa and has a pending green card application. The success of teachers like Ms. Mundo has two parts: both how they are screened and then how they are framed and supported. Filipino teachers at Central High School are far more likely to be successful at achieving their transnational migration goals, in part because Dr. Fielders screens for teachers advantaged by higher economic origins and better education as well as globally oriented social networks. Even among the economic improvement seekers, the teachers he selects are better positioned than the teachers who come from lower status universities and who have less of a global network. Ms. Mundo was able to borrow her placement fees interest-free from her U.S.–based brother; Ms. Cruz borrowed at high interest rates from a Philippines-based lender. These preexisting conditions positioned them differently in the migration process. Such variations even within the "migrating from" teachers highlight the complexity within the categories. However, their relative opportunity for success is further affected by the local framing of their school employers. The transient teacher mentality assumes short-term labor and minimizes investment in teacher adjustment. The transplant mentality is premised on retaining teachers and works to ensure their successful transition.

The consequences of these different experiences are not limited to the teachers. The implications for students in these two types of schools are markedly different and important.

Implications for Students and Schools

Ten of the twenty-four New Urban High School math teachers and ten of the thirty Central High School math teachers are from the Philippines. They were recruited overseas and hired in an effort to meet the demand for well-qualified math teachers in what are often called "hard-to-staff" schools. National and international reports, citing the relationship between teacher quality and student achievement, call for teachers with higher levels of math content knowledge as essential to improving students' math achievement.[5] The National Mathematics Advisory Council (NMAC) attributes a substantial part of the student variability in math achievement to teachers' math knowledge. Teachers' content knowledge is important in student learning. That being said, the council also acknowledges the difficulty of identifying measures and policy recommendations to guide the education and selection of teachers. Based on an analysis of twenty-seven years of research, the NMAC report concludes that there is more variability within teacher preparation pathways than between those pathways,[6] and that teacher content knowledge, not professional preparation pathway, is the most important differentiating factor in teacher effectiveness.

Although the NMAC report did not consider the transnational pathway in its analysis, that pathway bears out the within-pathway variation seen in other teacher preparation analysis. The stories of our two example schools, however, suggest the within-pathway variation may have as much to do with the schools themselves as it does with the teachers. All of the Filipino math teachers have degrees in mathematics, and many of them have advanced degrees. Given the claims about the relationship between teachers' math knowledge and student achievement, it would seem reasonable to expect both schools to have increased math scores along with their supply of well-qualified math teachers. This is not the case. Essentially, the students at Central High School have experienced substantial gains in their math scores since the recruitment of Filipino teachers, but the students at New Urban have not experienced similar gains. This within-pathway variation suggests more is involved than teacher content knowledge and that work context may be an equally important variable.

At New Urban High School, none of the math teachers have been there for more than three years. All of them are on J-1 cultural exchange visas and, while they hope to stay on beyond that with an H1B visa, that possibility seems uncertain. The school leaders have no real understanding of the teachers' visa situation, the teachers receive little adjustment support from the school, and frankly, no one is really looking to keep them. In an organization that accepts high turnover as the norm, replacing short-term teachers with other short-term teachers is business as usual; working to retain them is another way of operating altogether. No teachers or school administrators could give an exact number, but several reported first-year failure among the Filipino teachers as fairly common and attributed it to classroom management problems as well as failure to pass the state teacher exam. Many said that it was unfortunate, but none thought the school could do much to change it.

In contrast, of the ten Central High Math teachers, only one has been there for less than three years, while four have been there for eight years, and the rest fall in between. According to Dr. Fielders and several of the teachers, none of the Filipino teachers hired at Central have been lost to the school. All of them have successfully passed the state teacher exam, overcome classroom management challenges, and in most cases transitioned to a more permanent visa. Some have H1B labor shortage visas and two have been granted green cards. Again, the department head has been an important advocate in this process—supporting teachers' applications, advocating for the teachers at the district level, even finding a consulting attorney to guide them. Although visa sponsorship is not in the usual high school department head's job description, Dr. Fielders has taken it on as just another support system he must provide to retain his highly qualified teachers. He sees no other real alternative, as retaining highly qualified teachers, in his opinion, is responsible for the comparatively high student math achievement at Central High School: "Our math department triples the other ones around here [in student achievement]. *Triples.* And we still have 40 percent algebra failure."

On the California state math exam in 2008, 52 percent of Central High School's students were deemed proficient, up from just 10 percent in 2003 and 38 percent in 2005. Acknowledging that they as a school and a department still have a way to go to meet ongoing challenges,

Dr. Fielders also points out the higher achievement of his school compared with others like it in the district, as well as Central's steadily increasing math proficiency rates. He attributes the growing math achievement to the quality and stability of his math department—one-third of which is comprised of overseas trained Filipino teachers whom he describes as "rigorous, motivated, and focused," and he credits them substantially with the school's upward trajectory of math achievement.

In 2008, only 22 percent of New Urban High School's students achieved math proficiency, compared with 52 percent at Central High. Although markedly higher than the 9 percent deemed proficient in 2005—the school's first year, when it opened completely staffed with substitutes—it is still a far cry from the scores at Central High. Consider the difference in classroom terms. In a classroom of thirty students, proficiency could be expected from sixteen at Central High but only seven at New Urban. Each school serves thousands of students. At Central, 1,820 of the 3,500 students are achieving math proficiency; at New Urban, only 770 out of 3,500 are. Or, looked at the other way around, Central High has 1,680 students below proficiency, while New Urban High has 2,730 students below proficiency.

New Urban High School leaders describe their Filipino teachers as "compliant, complacent, and afraid to complain." and the hope is that they might successfully reach one or two students in their classrooms. As pointed out by school administrators, that is more than can be hoped for from the alternative—a substitute teacher lacking subject matter knowledge. High turnover is the accepted norm and is a reason to maintain close ties to new sources of teachers. Nearly half (10 of 24) of the New Urban math teachers are overseas trained Filipino teachers who have been on the faculty less than three years. Although New Urban is considered a comparable school to Central in student population, demographics, and size by both the district and the state, the two schools offer their students learning opportunities that are as different as the working environments that they offer their teachers. (See Table A.1 in the appendix for information on student demographics at each school.)

Issue can be taken with these numbers. Perhaps other things are at the root of the differential math achievement scores. Maybe the local elementary and middle schools that feed each of the high schools are offering vastly different learning opportunities. Maybe one school has a collaborative tutoring arrangement with a local university. Maybe environmental contaminants are worse in one neighborhood than the other, affecting student attention. There is no end to the possible conjectures accounting for the difference in the schools' scores.

What does stand, however, are the stated goals on the part of each school's leadership and the explanations they offer for their current realities. New Urban aims to reach one or two students per class—that being one or two more than an unqualified substitute might successfully teach. In this, it is exceeding its decidedly limited goals. Central High School intends, however, to achieve proficiency with all its students. In this ambitious goal, it is not yet wholly successful. In the striving, however, Central High is achieving math proficiency with notably more of its students than is New Urban High School. Furthermore, the Central High math department head credits the students' increasing achievement to the quality and stability of the school's math teachers. The two schools frame their teachers differently, aim for different goals with their students, and achieve different results in both areas. These two schools reflect different realities on making good on the promise of teachers with subject content knowledge.

Organizing for Teachers' Work

New Urban and Central High have organized themselves to attract and support different types of teachers, and they have obtained the teachers for whom they have organized. New Urban is organized for transient teachers, and it has transient teachers on its staff. Central is organized for transplant teachers, and it has transplant teachers on its staff. It is not simple to determine which came first—the structural organization or the teacher type. The process reflects a reciprocal series of events. What is clear, however, is that a school organized for transience is not going to cultivate transplant. While the transient orientation may have resulted from high teacher turnover, the school will continue to have a transient teacher population as long as that is its operating frame. Schools get the teachers for whom they organize.

What does it mean to organize for transience or organize for transplant? While some of the differences between New Urban and Central High are perhaps quite amorphous—conceptions of what it means to be a teacher and what constitutes good teaching are often viewed as gray areas—other variations are decidedly tangible and identifiable. What each school's leaders knew about candidates prior to hiring, the teachers' preview of the schools and work, the new teacher supports and attitude toward induction, and the structure and position of school leadership in relation to the teachers are markedly different at the two schools and have decided effects on the schools' teacher workforce. It is one thing to say a school frames teachers as transients or transplants—and another thing altogether to identify some of the structural elements that both result from and create those framings.

Job Preview

As indicated at the start of this chapter, job preview is considered important in facilitating a successful match between schools and teachers.[7] The more a school knows about a teacher prior to hiring and the more a teacher knows about a school, the more likely it is that the two will be well matched, the placement will stick, and both will be satisfied. Such previews help improve teacher retention and increase the chances that a teacher will stay and take root at a school rather than pass quickly through it. A factor that increases job preview—decentralized and information–rich hiring practices—is practiced more routinely at Central High than at New Urban. The district itself has made efforts to decentralize hiring, but it cannot control what happens at the school level. District human resource personnel do the initial screening of teachers to create a qualified pool from which local schools can hire, and the schools take it from there.

Preview has little meaning at New Urban because the pool of applicants is tiny and often the only alternative is a short-term substitute and the need to hire pressing. Typically, New Urban hires Filipino teachers at a district school fair, far from the school and classroom. A single vice principal makes a hiring decision based on a five-minute interview. The New Urban principal, Mr. Cortez, says openings at his school rarely receive more than one applicant, and frequently that candidate is a Filipino teacher. An overseas trained teacher with a preliminary credential is preferable to a substitute teacher with no subject knowledge. The school must also face the reality that substitutes can turn over every few weeks, while overseas trained teachers are likely to stay for at least a year. The school leaders hiring an OTT know little beyond the teacher's name, subject area, and credential status. The teacher accepts the position based on nothing more than the five-minute interview, the personality of the interviewer, and the need to secure a position. Both the interviewer and the applicant are desperate, and the two latch onto one another quickly, forced to make a decision based on little information.

At Central High School, the hiring process permitted more preview in both directions. Hiring of Filipino math teachers at Central has had two major iterations, both orchestrated by the math department head. For his first overseas hires, he selected initial interviewees based on his personal knowledge of the Philippines and the candidates' education and employment history as indicators of quality. He interviewed candidates on-site at the school and provided information on his professional expectations and the student body, and he conducted a tour of the school facilities. Other hires have been done through recommendations from his current teachers, meaning that the first few hires become the source for networked recruitment. Prospective teachers learned about the school and the conditions there through their friends working there, and the department head learned about prospective new math teachers through trusted current math teachers. He had the luxury of choice, which permitted him and the teachers the time and space needed to engage in information rich decentralized hiring practices.

New Teacher Supports

It is now widely understood that supporting new teachers increases their satisfaction, effectiveness, and retention. Teachers who receive no professional induction support turn over at much higher rates than teachers who receive a full spectrum of induction support.[8] In particular, mentorships with teachers in the same field, shared planning time with colleagues, new teacher seminars, collegial support networks, good administrator communication, and help from a teacher's aide are all effective tools individually but collectively make for a powerful induction package. New Urban High School delivers none of these elements, while Central delivers all of them.

New teacher induction is part of California's two step credential process. The preliminary credential is cleared by fulfilling additional requirements, which include completing the Beginning Teacher Support and Assessment (BTSA) program, receiving positive local evaluations, passing all state exams, and sometimes—as in the case of special education teachers—completing additional professional development units. While the OTTs are not new to teaching, they are new to the California teaching credential system. Like any other new teacher, they must clear their preliminary credential—only the stakes are even higher for them. Failure to clear the preliminary credential by the end of a teacher's first year means no contract renewal. Failure to complete BTSA by the end of the three-year visa means no chance of additional visa sponsorship. The two case study schools differ greatly in their approach to new teacher induction.

New Urban High School takes a hands-off approach to new teacher support. They offer BTSA and it is available to teachers who seek it out, but they do not require teachers to participate in it nor do they even go to any length to ensure that teachers know how or why to access it. The Filipino teachers there remarked repeatedly in interviews that they were surprised by the credential requirements, didn't understand until it was too late that they had to complete the requirements, and generally felt confused and uncertain about the BTSA program. Meanwhile, New Urban's BTSA coordinator complained that the school's Filipino teachers had not sought her out for support. As the principal there said, "Some of the teachers that I have have not fulfilled the requirements that the district has set forth for them to do for their teaching credential." At New Urban, any support received is support sought actively by the teacher. Those who do not know where to seek it, or do not understand its importance, just do not receive it.

In contrast, Central High School requires all of its new teachers, including its overseas trained Filipino teachers, to participate in an array of new teacher supports, including BTSA. None of it is optional. All new teachers must follow the routine: attend a monthly meeting, serve as a teaching assistant in a more experienced teacher's classroom, have a more experienced teacher serve as a teaching assistant in their classroom, and meet with the full department for collective planning. New teachers are also observed by and meet with their department head routinely. At Central High, school leaders, especially in the form of department heads, act as the stewards of new teacher support and development.

Leadership and Structure

Given that Central High School and New Urban High School approach job preview and new teacher induction quite differently, it is not surprising that they also have markedly different leadership and structural styles regarding teachers' work. These differences have implications for the work orientations and experiences of the OTTs. The schools differ in the degree to which they organize themselves around subject departments and the subject expertise of the leaders most proximal to teacher hiring, professional development, and assessment. Subject-based leadership, versus more generalized leadership, has very different traditions, structural systems in schools, and implications for teachers' work.

Although both leadership forms—the subject-based and more general— are found in secondary schools, organizing to favor one over the other influences how teachers approach their work and how schools are positioned to support teachers' work. Schools that have shifted to the more general orientations tend to see a school and teacher level focus on universal goals, like personalizing the curriculum or reducing incidents of failing marks across the whole school. Whereas, schools in which the leadership is subject-focused tend to have better supports for subject specific pedagogical practice.[9]

New Urban High School is organized into houses—schools within schools that cluster teachers across subjects and organize students into smaller learning communities, often with the goal of personalizing the school (i.e., making a large school feel smaller) and structuring the learning around some shared thematic topic, often an occupational interest. This model is generally adopted with students in mind, and yet it also alters teachers' experiences of the schools, particularly as it pertains to the leaders most proximal to teachers. In the case of New Urban, a school vice-principal who has direct oversight of the teachers and students in his or her house leads each house. Departments cut across the houses and department heads are leaders mostly in name. School meetings and the organization of learning occur in houses. The leader most directly responsible for teacher supervision is unlikely to share subject matter affiliations or to attend to subject pedagogical practice.

This was highlighted at a house meeting that was intentionally scheduled by vice-principal David Thomas, a former social studies teacher, in Alma Cruz's classroom. The VP elected to host a house meeting in Alma Cruz's room in order to showcase what he considered to be admirable wall displays of students' work. He joked that he didn't know what half of the math meant but thought everyone could learn something from Alma about how to create a beautiful classroom. In this model, teacher leadership does not presume or require subject matter knowledge.

At Central High School, as has already been well established in this chapter, teachers' work is lead and stewarded by department heads. Dr. Fielders, the math department head, is the undisputed leader of his department, both structurally and in terms of knowledge and experience. He has taught longer than anyone there, has a higher level of math education than any other math teacher, and leads the department. By his own definition, he is a true subject leader, being both an administrator and a subject specialist:

I run my department as I did when I was back East as a department chair . . . That is, as an administrator. Back East, department chairs are administrators. We are just like APs, in fact, it is even worse because not only do you have to have your credential for first- and second-tier administration, but you had to also have, in order to be a department chair, a master's in your field. You can be an AP without a master's degree.

Dr. Fielders prides himself on having built and developed what he considers to be "one of the top math departments around." He did so in large part because creating a strong math department was how he defined his primary mission as math department head. The teachers who work for him are led by an expert who can guide them in their subject matter and pedagogical practice.

New Urban and Central High offer very different working environments for teachers—both overseas and domestic—and each school has gotten the teachers for whom they have organized.

In Sum

The two schools discussed in this chapter provide two orientations toward teachers and their work, and two different realities have been the result. Certainly, the position of teachers and their reasons for migration affect their experience of transnational labor migration, and those effects can be exacerbated or mediated by their experiences in American schools. Transient schools become magnets for the least empowered OTTs, framing them and treating them like short-term labor, exploiting their migration aspirations; these schools practically ensure the teachers' failure to thrive. They hire teachers because they need someone who meets the on-paper subject specialism qualifications to fill a spot in a classroom.

In contrast, transplant schools are both more appealing to teachers who are in a position to be selective and are generally more selective themselves. Transplant schools carefully choose each teacher they hire with an eye toward building its faculty, and they then invest in teacher development and retention. Teachers who aspire to stay find the infrastructure and support they need to stay at transplant schools.

These conditions are relevant for more than the OTTs. That there are "best of times" schools for teachers, transnational and otherwise, and for students is compelling reason to seek these conditions for all teachers,

American and overseas trained, and for all U.S. students. Based on the teachers interviewed and schools visited for this research, New Urban is the norm and Central the exception when it comes to the workplaces of OTTs.

Overseas trained teachers, however, are not creating the high transiency rate in U.S. schools—rather, they are considered viable employment options in many U.S. schools because short-term, subject specialism has come to be an accepted norm in many schools. No Child Left Behind focused attention on the individual characteristics of teachers, not on the school's collective capacity given its overall constellation of teacher labor. The legislation seeks evidence that each teacher individually has subject matter and grade level expertise. It does not require that schools stabilize their workforce by attaining an optimal teacher turnover rate, and it does not consider the organizational ratio of sources for qualified teachers (intern program, university, Teach for America, etc.). NCLB does not consider the organizational profile of teacher seniority as an aspect of quality, and it does not concern itself with the cultural affinity of teachers with student populations.

The No Child Left Behind Act does not ask for evidence of organizational capacity. Consequently, a school with 75 percent first-year credentialed teachers and a 60 percent turnover rate is considered equal to a school with an evenly distributed range of teacher experience and a 10 percent turnover rate—despite the documented relationship between high teacher turnover and low student achievement.[10] NCLB has focused attention on short-term individual teacher-level academic criteria of qualifications without attending to other significant aspects of ensuring a qualified—and high quality—evenly distributed teacher workforce. Collective capacity has been overlooked in the emphasis on individual qualifications.

The next chapter takes up the question of what all of this means to and for the teaching profession, including conceptions of teachers' work, student experience, and the schools of industrialized countries. It positions the findings of this book in current understandings of teachers work, and expands those conceptions through the contribution of these findings.

PART THREE

Implications

6

TEACHERS' WORK

Teachers are on the move.

Teachers are moving between countries to meet labor market needs. They are moving from developing to industrialized countries. They are moving from the schools and students of their homelands to the schools and students of countries that can pay them higher wages. They are moving from one teaching specialization into another—some of them are even moving into teaching—in order to move between countries.

These movements are relatively new and part of a postindustrialized period of labor migration. Ten years ago, a few teachers might move to another country for a short adventure, or they might marry and make a more permanent move. Some teachers moved to developing countries to aid in educational infrastructure—for example, when the Thomasites went to the Philippines. But mass movements of teachers across national borders for the intentional purpose of work are unprecedented and, arguably, contributing to the suppressed status of the teaching profession.

These movements represent a departure from the traditional emphasis of teachers as homegrown stalwarts of their communities and purveyors of cultural capital to the next generation of their own citizens.[1] Teaching can no longer be seen as the local work done by those most motivated by the intrinsic rewards of student and community development. Instead, a growing number of teachers are global workers whose employment patterns are driven by the market demands and purchase power of schools and nations. They are guest workers—brought in on temporary work visas to do the work unfilled by local labor markets. They go where the money is and teach the children of nations and schools that can best afford them.

These movements are, in part, a result of changed definitions of what it means to be a teacher. The teaching profession is being redefined;

especially in many industrialized countries, the expectations of teachers are narrower than they have been historically. These changes make teachers' movements more possible. And, in moving, teachers are reshaping the contours of the teaching profession and creating a newly conceived and enacted notion of a transnational teacher.

Teacher Migration and Labor Queues

Intentional teacher labor migration to industrialized countries emerged as part of the postindustrial migration period that began in the 1960s. Movements from densely settled developing countries to densely settled industrialized countries characterize postindustrial migration. In contrast, labor migration flows of the industrial era (1800–1925) drew people from densely to sparsely settled industrialized countries—for example, as happened with the European immigrants settling in North America and New Zealand. These almost uniform flows of immigrants to former colonies were replaced in the postindustrial period with flows out of developing countries to industrialized ones (Massey et al., 2008; Castles & Miller, 2009). This trend so profoundly shifted migration patterns that some European sending countries became receiving countries as the formerly colonized became the source of secondary labor in the segmented labor market of industrialized economies.

Flows of teachers from developing countries like the Philippines to industrialized ones like the United States have animated this postindustrialized period. These flows are at least partially explained by segmented labor market theory arguing that labor demands of industrialized countries drive immigration. Segmented labor theory explains immigration from developing to industrialized countries in this postindustrial period as stemming from employers needs for workers to fill jobs at the bottom of the occupational hierarchy. An unwillingness to increase wages or improve working conditions, as well as a desire for flexibility in reducing labor costs during economic downturns, drives employer demand for immigrant workers who have minimal rights and see bottom-level jobs as a means of earning money regardless of the employment uncertainty or working conditions. Essentially, segmented labor theory explains the demand by industrialized countries for immigrant labor as the need on the part of employers in the industrialized country to sustain a source of low status disempowered workers.[2]

Consistent with segmented labor queue theory is job queue theory as an explanation of within nation distribution of workers and jobs. Job queue theory contends that all economies have a hierarchical ladder of preferable jobs and a parallel ladder of preferable workers. The assumption is that a hierarchical distribution of jobs and workers occurs in which the best workers get the best jobs leaving the lowest rung jobs for the lowest workers. Worker position, however, is not simply tied to productivity or education. Gender in particular can place workers lower on the worker ladder, and occupations can be demoted on the ladder through feminization. Job queue theory notes the existence of status differentials across and within occupations and confirms the need for a supply of bottom-rung workers to fill bottom-rung jobs.[3]

Job queue theory helps to illuminate teaching as a bottom-rung professional occupation populated by bottom-rung professional workers. Workers with the fewest occupational options—namely, women and African Americans—have historically populated teaching. Within the teaching occupation, there is an even further hierarchical distribution of jobs with those schools noted as "hard to staff" accessing the least qualified workers. Those bottom-rung schools have long relied on workers at the bottom of the teacher queue by hiring underqualified and newly qualified teachers such as interns and emergency credentialed and novice teachers.[4]

These bottom-rung workers became a less viable option for hard to staff schools when the No Child Left Behind legislation increased the employer costs of hiring underqualified teachers. This legislation essentially cut off employers' ability to rely on this particular pool of bottom-rung workers. Segmented labor theory explains why schools then looked overseas for another source of low status, bottom of the ladder teachers. The alternative would have required schools to increase wages and improve working conditions to increase the occupational status of working in these "hard to staff" schools. Securing a new immigrant source of bottom-rung teachers, motivated by the opportunity to earn income regardless of the working conditions and low status of the work, suppressed the need to make occupational changes to the reward structure or status of the teaching profession.

Teachers as Guest Workers

Guest work is, by its very definition and nature, bottom-rung work. Nations invite guest workers only when they are unable to fill jobs deemed undesirable by higher status native-born workers. Teachers are not the first category of guest workers, either in the United States or elsewhere, and much of their experience is predicated on the experience of guest workers that came before them. Looking at earlier guest worker experiences highlights the importance of understanding both the source of, and interaction of, migrant motivations and the framing and reception of the local receiving community. Success is mediated both by why people migrate and how they are received—and the interaction of the two.

The United States has long drawn on the global market to supply its farm workers, and more recently nannies, hospitality workers, nurses, and high tech workers. There is a large body of research—historical, economic, sociological, and anthropological—that documents and explores the experiences of these other types of guest workers, especially those of farm workers and, to a lesser extent, nurses. This work informs the experiences of guest worker teachers, and, while limited, the research specific to teachers' migration indicates that the findings of this book have relevance beyond the specific circumstances of the cases presented here. As shown by the historical and contemporary experiences of migrant employment, guest worker teachers are influencing what it means to be a teacher in industrialized countries by helping to frame teaching jobs as lower rung, temporary, single focus, interchangeable, and culturally and relationally neutral.

Guest Work as Low-Status Work

By definition, guest workers are foreign nationals who enter the United States officially for a predefined period of time to do specific work. Typically, the U.S. Congress authorizes guest worker visas and programs when the Department of Labor is convinced that a critical national labor shortage exists. Many contend that these labor shortages have more to do with pay and working conditions than they do with an actual shortage of workers. What is consistent across guest workers, though, is that they are doing the work that Americans opt not to do. This typically includes work that is considered low-status, poorly paid, dangerous, unpleasant, or, all of the above. Of course, Americans also fill these occupations—but guest worker programs are premised on the notion that not enough Americans can or will fill the labor demand—at least at the wages and working conditions offered.[5]

Historically, guest work nets mixed results for the workers themselves. Migration may increase the economic or social status of workers in their country of origin—but in the United States, guest worker status may simultaneously place them in a vulnerable position of low status and few enforceable rights. For example, higher earnings in the United States may go far in supporting families left in the country of origin—but workers who complain about working conditions often find themselves quickly repatriated.[6] Since guest workers are sponsored by individual employers or consortiums of employers, for guest workers, employment is the key to their visas. Losing employment means losing the right to stay. Successful guest workers—those who stay the course—learn to work within the conditions they encounter.

In some cases, guest workers may springboard their short-term work earnings into new business opportunities once they return home. Alvaro Garcia, a Braceros program farm worker, opened a barbershop with his savings earned as a guest worker.[7] He slept in barracks, stayed far from his family, worked long hours in American fields, and saved enough to buy land and open a barbershop upon his return. He lived a successful transnational version of the immigrant story—hard work, sacrifice, and opportunity leading to improved circumstances back home. Not everyone fares as well, however. Guest worker chances for success are based, in part, on external factors that have little to do with their own determination, hard work, or motivation. How guest workers, as a class, are framed and perceived in the employing community is an important element over which the workers themselves have little influence.

The Consequences of Worker Reception

Local reception influences worker success. Workers who are framed by the local labor community as essential and important to the success of the community, and perhaps even the nation, are more likely to be well received. A good reception helps ensure successful labor migration, while a poor reception can negate the chances of even the most determined individual. Comparing farm work and teaching may seem a poor match; however, the two are quite alike when worker reception is considered. Teachers in transplant-oriented schools are more successful than teachers in transient-oriented schools. Similarly, farm workers ascribed a higher status during reception are more successful than those locally framed as last resorts.

During World War II, for example, Jamaican guest farm workers were welcomed as heroes sent to save the crops from rotting in the fields in the northern United States. In the southern United States, however, they were treated like regular black American workers of the time—

treated badly and subject to segregation and discrimination in the South. In some northern cities, Jamaican guest workers were granted keys to the city and memberships to country clubs. In most southern states, the Jamaican farm workers were seen as more low-wage black labor, treated as poorly as black Americans of the time, and forced to sign "Jim Crow creed" agreements. Not surprisingly, Jamaican workers experienced far greater work success in the northern states than in the southern states. As a result, hundreds of Jamaican workers were deported from southern states in the first few weeks of their time there.[8]

Nursing is both similar to and different from farm work migrations. Nurses, like farm workers, have their own visa category. Many nurses also leave their families behind in their home countries while they support them from their guest worker positions.[9] However, Braceros were all male guest workers—by policy. Guest worker nurses are mostly female—by profession—and they are working in a professional rather than manual labor category. These two distinctions are important variations, which make nursing a closer match case to teaching. Both teaching and nursing are primarily and historically feminized, low status, semi-professional occupations.

Parallels between Nursing and Teaching

Nursing and teaching are professional labor categories that require advanced education and skills. Visa approval is dependent on nurses and teachers demonstrating that they have the education and experience required to merit admission. This means that, unlike farm work, in which the criteria for entry were fixed (gender, physical fitness, and the indication that they were willing to take instruction), nursing can attract people into the profession who seek to migrate as guest workers. For some, the nursing degree is a professional passport to migration more than an occupational interest in its own right. Transnational migration becomes, then, a reason for occupational selection.

Nursing's status as a profession, however, does not ensure favorable working conditions any more than it does for teachers. Similar to teachers, guest worker nurses lose their right to remain in the United States when they lose their employment. This connection between employment and immigration status undermines workers' voices, creating conditions that allow for labor exploitation. The likelihood of exploitation is increased when the nurses do not have viable home country labor options because of limited labor opportunities, below-sustenance wage levels, or other adversity that makes home return unlikely. Without the choice to leave unfavorable working situations, guest worker nurses accept working conditions that would be deemed intolerable by others.[10]

In essence, guest worker nurses, especially those with few alternative options, become a labor source for the positions other nurses eschew. Homegrown "domestically sourced" nurses, as well as the nurses whose work travel is motivated more by adventure and exploration, as opposed to need and deprivation, are able to be more selective in their working conditions and situations.

In parallel circumstances with guest worker nurses, guest worker teachers gain increased earnings that may help them achieve their financial goals—yet, along with the increased earnings comes an ironic decrease in occupational status. South African teachers in England quickly learn that they are there to teach in the low socioeconomic neighborhoods where headmasters are unable to attract and retain British teachers. Filipino teachers in the United States learn that they are expected to teach in the "hell" schools. In both situations, the teachers are primarily framed as short term, high turnover solutions in schools that frame them as transient.

The few studies that consider teachers' experience in the England to South Africa migration do not explicitly use the lens of "reception" to make sense of the experience of OTTs in England. Reception, however, is the best lens with which to examine what these teachers experience. Most teachers report teaching in schools with poor student discipline and an overall lack of work ethic. They quickly come to see themselves, based on their experience of how they are locally framed and placed, as occupying the bottom of the occupational and social status ladder. This in turn affects how they engage with their work and their likelihood of success. When they see themselves and their students as abandoned together at the bottom of the ladder, transnational teachers are inclined toward early departure or detachment. On the other hand, school recognition and support for their efforts reinforces their resolve to stay, engage, and succeed.

Similarly, research on the successful transition of OTTs in the United States indicates that these teachers need specialized and targeted support. A study of new teacher induction found that the mentorship support provided to novice teachers is not the best support for teachers who are new to the country but not new to teaching. These teachers, the research contends, need cultural and social adjustment with pedagogical implications, not the basics of how to teach.[11]

The work of Manik, Maharaj, and Sookrajh bears this out. They report extreme culture shock among the overwhelming majority of South African teachers newly arrived in England's classrooms. Most were left to find their own way—and while some navigate the adjustment well, other highly trained and experienced teachers do not.[12] As the research in California demonstrates, when left alone in a sink-or-swim situation, the vast majority of transnational teachers are likely to return home without successfully adapting to their new work environment

It is clear that subject matter training and years of teaching experience are not the only predictors of success for transnational teachers. Increasingly, however, the important factors of reception, targeted support, and guest worker status are ignored in favor of a narrow emphasis on subject specialism. This emphasis is not simply a driver of demand for transnational teachers; it also strongly influences their potential effectiveness and success as teachers.

Narrowing Teachers' Work

Transnational teacher migration is part of a distinct trend in the teaching profession. Especially in many industrialized countries, definitions of teachers' work have emphasized subject specialism and de-emphasized other aspects of teachers' work—the work of caring for students' personal and emotional development, the work of being a role model and an established and constant adult presence in the community, the work of serving as a conduit to knowledge and opportunity in higher education and career opportunities, as well as the work of cultivating citizenship.[13]

Reforms targeted at improving the academic excellence and equity patterns of student learning have led countries such as the United States and England to embrace and enact a standards and accountability approach to schooling. This approach defines learning outcomes and measures them on high stakes tests—high stakes for students, teachers, and schools. In this system, qualified teachers know their subject, and effective teaching has come to mean high student scores on standardized tests. This definition makes the need to attract teachers with academic content knowledge the most highlighted aspect of school staffing. Academic content knowledge gets prioritized over other, arguably equally important, aspects of teachers' work. This marginalizes the relational and cultural aspects of teachers' work—aspects of teachers' work that deserve equal billing in conceptions of what it means to be a qualified teacher.

Cultural Affinity

Despite the widespread observation that structural features of schooling have achieved a certain institutional isomorphism,[14] the daily work of teaching also reflects quite localized notions of what teachers and children are expected to do and achieve in classrooms, as well as the relationships teachers are expected to form with colleagues, administrators, parents, and the community. Teaching skills are not as directly transferable between nations as transnational teacher recruitment practices suggest. Although there are certainly similarities found in national approaches to schooling, there are also significant pedagogical differences in expectations, approaches, norms, and interpersonal relationships between teachers and students. These differences affect how teachers work and how they expect to work, what they deem good practice and how they engage with students.[15]

For example, Anderson-Levitt's comparative study of first-grade classrooms in France and the United States shows considerable differences in teachers' ideas regarding the appropriate behavior of six-year-olds, and in the practices the teachers employed in teaching those six-year-olds to read. In a video-based component of the study, Anderson-Levitt found that teachers from each country recognized similarities in each other's classroom environments, but they also expressed substantial surprise. For example, American teachers were surprised to see the use of cursive writing in French first-grade classrooms, judging six-year-olds not "ready" for cursive; French teachers were surprised to see American six-year-olds grouped together on a rug for reading time, viewing that as a practice to be left behind when children entered the "real work" of first grade.[16]

Anderson-Levitt asks the question: "what about the transnational, even universal, knowledge for teaching that many scholars seem to take for granted?" Her answer is to acknowledge parallel aspects of school organization (both countries group six-year-olds together for instruction in what is termed first grade) and point to "professional know-how" that reflects a transnational understanding of classroom culture. She also offers this argument: "Teachers are similar across national boundaries only at a high level of abstraction. Most of the professional knowledge shared across national boundaries remains open-ended, abstract, and bland until filled in with nation-specific details."[17]

Similarly, Alexander introduces his five-nation study of primary education by observing, "Though a few comparative studies have ranged convincingly over several countries, [such studies] concentrate their attention on the macro or national level and say little about the day-to-day workings of schools, still less hazard analysis of pedagogy." He continues his argument:

> Though there are undoubted cross-cultural continuities and indeed universals in educational thinking and practice, no decision or action which one observes in a particular classroom . . . can be properly understood except by reference to the web of inherited ideas and values, habits and customs, institutions and world views which make one country, or one region, or one group, distinct from another.[18]

Differences in culturally specific frames of reference for teaching, together with the absence of community knowledge and connections, thus seem likely to present challenges to the sense of efficacy experienced by OTTs. And yet, in recruiting teachers from overseas, teaching work is presented as culturally neutral—transferable between communities, cultures, and countries. That a newly arrived OTT can be expected to take full and immediate charge of a classroom in the United States is a reflection of the presumed cultural neutrality and transferability of teaching work. The example of a South African teacher's conscious avoidance of student behavior problems demonstrates how the cultural differences play out in the relational aspects of teachers' work. Teaching work is far from culturally neutral—even within a nation, there is a need for a culturally relevant pedagogical practice to help ensure student success. The idea is not that teacher and students must be culturally identical or even a close match—but rather that teachers must be knowledgeable of and take into account their students' histories, current realities, and social and linguistic norms and traditions. Teachers lacking a cultural frame of reference for their students are less effective at teaching them academic content.[19]

Relational Aspects of Teaching

Teachers do more than teach subject matter. They have long been framed in the United States as of and from the local community in which they teach. Motivated by a desire to improve the lives of children, teachers are typically believed to have more in common with ministers than accountants in their line of work—it is more a calling that an occupation.

Teaching is seen by many as a calling to serve and improve their communities.

That teachers are an embedded feature of their communities is revealed in the demographic data on teacher labor patterns as well as in community practices and teacher policy. Most first-time teachers take up a post at a school within twenty-five miles of where they themselves went to high school: Teachers are notable for their desire, expressed from a young age, to find work in their local communities.[20] They are expected to be role models to children and to steward their personal and moral development. They are also supposed to teach, both by example and through the curriculum, what it means to be a member of that community. Perhaps nowhere is that more apparent than in the long-standing policy of some states requiring teachers to be U.S. citizens. Teachers are expected to help "Americanize" students—to help them acclimatize to the culture, values, and conventions of American society. Teachers do instruct students in an academic discipline, yet they are also purveyors of social and cultural capital.

The quest for subject specialism has marginalized attention to these relational aspects of teachers' work. This manifests itself in an overattention to assessing teachers' effectiveness through students' test scores and an underattention to teachers' effectiveness at connecting with students and engaging them with their school and community environments. This focus can result in the underappreciation of relationally effective teachers—especially in schools where that success is often hard-won.

Consider Rigoberto Ruelas, a Los Angeles teacher at Miramonte Elementary School—known for his success reaching out to gang-affiliated youth—was publicly labeled as "less effective" because of his students' low standardized math test scores. When his students did not score as well as other students on the state standardized math exam, the *Los Angeles Times* published, in 2010, the scores and the related teacher effectiveness ratings. Ruelas's despondency at his "less effective" rating, and his suicide not long after, sparked a public debate as to the appropriateness of teacher ratings based on student tests. A newspaper spokesperson contended that the newspaper published the ratings because "it bears directly on the performance of public employees who provide an important service, and in the belief that parents and the public have a right to judge the data for themselves."[21] The teachers' union countered that, though the test results were but one measure of teacher effectiveness, the *Times* article elevated them to a more universal status. *The Huffington Post* did a follow-up article that cited former students on the relational effectiveness of Ruelas:

> By all accounts, he was a dedicated teacher who cared deeply about the children at Miramonte. Parents and students said he often stayed after school to tutor struggling kids and offer counseling so they stayed on the straight and narrow.
>
> "He took the worse students and tried to change their lives," said Delgado, the former student. "I had friends who wanted to be gangsters, but he talked them out of it. He treated you like family."
>
> Parents said they were grateful.
>
> "He gave my son good advice. He told him to study and to listen to his parents," said Guadelupe Pina, whose son was in Ruelas' class last year.[22]

Ruelas came out of the same community in which he taught. In the face of poor student behavior he did not, as the South African teacher in London did, "put his hands in his pockets and think of the pounds." Instead, he engaged fully with his students, showing them how he cared about them and helping them navigate their way in the world. Arguably, relational effectiveness alone is no more sufficient than academic effectiveness alone in assessing teachers. Academic effectiveness, though, has eclipsed considerations of relational effectiveness.

Overseas trained teachers represent a divergence from the tradition of local teachers of and from the community. Not only are they not from the community in which they teach, they are recruited to do the work that no one from the community is willing or able to do. Instead of being local role models, they are guest workers paid to do a discrete set of tasks and broadly understood to be motivated by the extrinsic rewards of higher pay. This diverges from the traditional model and ignores the relational aspects of teachers' work.

The Many Dimensions of Highly Qualified Teachers

The push for highly qualified teachers is intended to ensure that all students get access to a well-educated teacher who is knowledgeable in his or her subject area. In the United States, that push is nationally embodied in the No Child Left Behind Act of 2001. Although this legislation

mandates that U.S. states ensure that their teachers have subject expertise, it does not specify the importance of the cultural or relational
aspects of teachers' work, highlighting instead the rational, definable,
and measurable elements. It offers a definition of highly qualified teachers
that is premised on a culturally neutral set of skills that can be drawn on
and delivered equally well in any context.

Cochran-Smith and Lytle challenge the technical framing of the No
Child Left Behind Act as lacking the contextual and relational aspects of
high quality teaching.[23] Teaching work, they contend, is messy. It does
not lend itself well to mandates and regulations. They challenge the notion
of teacher quality as based on decontextualized external expertise—
calling instead for definitions of teacher quality that acknowledges the
importance of teacher connection to students and location within the
community.

Ladson-Billing has conducted work on culturally relevant pedagogy
and has presented an additional case of teacher quality as embedded in
the local community.[24] She studied individuals locally defined as high-
quality teachers for African American students. Eight teachers were
identified in lists of teachers generated by both parents and administrators, and all eight agreed to the three-year study. The teachers were all
women; three of them were white, five were African American, and six
were from working-class backgrounds. Rather than finding common
teaching practices or even styles, she discovered that the commonalities
were how teachers saw their work as teachers and how they thought
about their students. She frames culturally relevant teaching as being a
social and political advocate and resource for students. In particular, she
defines "highly qualified" teachers for African-American students as
teachers with cultural capital and political power.

Identifying highly qualified teachers according to subject matter
training alone ignores important relational and cultural roles and factors
that contribute to successful teaching. Expertise in subject matter alone
is not sufficient for preparing transnational teachers for success in the
classroom. Yet a narrow emphasis on subject matter training requirements for transnational teachers persists. This narrow emphasis is facilitated by an emerging framing of teaching as a culturally neutral transfer
of knowledge. This reframing of teaching is reshaping the contours of
what it means to be a teacher.

Teaching itself is on the move. The notion of a culturally neutral, transnational teacher is generating some unusual phenomena. In addition to

teachers moving from their countries to teach, several efforts are underway to draw on teacher subject knowledge without moving the teacher. Indian tutors are now available online for personal study support, and many schools are experimenting with Internet-based classes. The most extreme example, though, is in the emerging South Korean teacher robots.

South Korean engineers developed a remote-controlled teaching robot that is operated from afar. In early pilots, a teacher in the Philippines operates the robot. She teaches English to students in South Korea via her telepresence in a penguin-shaped, rolling robot with flashing lights. Her voice is transmitted and her facial expressions are used to animate the movements of the robot's avatar face. South Korea hopes to soon have one in every kindergarten classroom, and they are working on a model that will function without a human teacher operator.[25] *Time* magazine named the English-teaching robots one of the fifty best inventions of 2010 and reported that "experts say the bots could eventually phase out flesh-and-blood foreign English teachers altogether."[26]

The notion of teaching as knowledge transfer, culturally neutral, and distinct from student-teacher relationships allows for the projection of a teacher's voice and face from a computer lab in one country into a robot in the classroom of another country. This is an extreme manifestation of a strictly subject specialist conception of teacher quality. Teachers as short-term guest workers are another manifestation of a narrow conception of teachers' work.

7

TRANSNATIONAL TEACHER MIGRATION

Overseas trained teachers are an established part of the U.S. teacher labor market. Debates can ensue as to their relative effectiveness at teaching American students, the role they play in the labor market, and the implications for the teaching profession. That there are overseas trained teachers in U.S. schools, however, is a fact.

At a time when low-income urban U.S. schools experienced a demand for subject specialist teachers, overseas trained teachers, especially those from developing countries, emerged as a supply source of teachers. The U.S. demand for transnational teachers with subject specialism emerges from a policy context of academic standards and accountability that privileges teacher content knowledge over both cultural affinity and the relational aspects of teachers' work. As a result, math, science, and special education teachers have been a focus of major recruitment efforts.

The migration of teachers into the United States has been facilitated by an immigration context that permits labor visas for short-term labor solutions and is informed by a long-standing American orientation to the global market for certain types of mostly low-status labor. Overseas trained teachers have become a significant and expanding source of teachers in the United States that, for too long, has gone relatively unexamined.

This utilization of the overseas labor market for teacher supply appeared in the United States in the urban areas of New York, Texas, and California, and it was later adopted as a response to demand in places such as Georgia and Maryland. While not comprising a large percentage of teachers overall, the numbers of OTTs sought by U.S. schools far exceeds other alternative supply sources such as Teach for America. And like Teach for America teachers, migrant teachers are concentrated in the schools at the bottom rung of the U.S. teacher employment options.

There are two major categories of overseas trained teachers in the United States: teachers migrating to adventure and travel opportunities, and teachers migrating from economic and social constraints.

For transnational teachers from other industrialized countries, migration is predominately an opportunity for travel, adventure, and cultural exchange. They are migrating to something and risk little in their movements. For example, the teachers from Spain have options—jobs waiting for them back home that pay adequately—and those options give them a voice in their migration. These teachers embrace their short-term visas and intend to go home after enjoying an extended working holiday.

For transnational teachers from developing countries, migration is an opportunity for gains in economics and social status as well as an opportunity to move away from poverty and deprivation. The results, however, can be lower status, difficult working conditions, and economic hardship. When OTTs are migrating from deprivation and disadvantage, returning home is not an easy option. Many migrant teachers aspire to stay in the new country and, consequently, they are willing to endure poor working conditions and treatment in order to retain their overseas posts and visas.

In the case of teacher migration from the Philippines to California, teachers are seen as guest workers and their local reception has a significant effect on their chances for success in placement schools. Schools that frame and treat transnational teachers as transient have higher teacher turnover at the schools and are at greater risk of low student achievement. Schools that frame and treat transnational teachers as transplants, as individuals who can and will stay as part of the teaching faculty, have lower teacher turnover at the school level and have increased student achievement patterns. A transplant orientation to transnational teacher migration appears to be a good option for the U.S. schools that employ these teachers and the students they serve.

U.S. schools that draw on the overseas market as a short-term, high-turnover labor market solution can disadvantage their students, and perhaps the teaching profession, by emphasizing supply-side rather than demand-side solutions. Furthermore, the contours of the teaching profession are affected by teacher migration, altering who enters teaching, why they enter, and where they teach.

Transplanting Teachers

Transplanting overseas teachers is better for the students in America's high poverty urban schools than a transient orientation to transnational teacher employment, which undermines the organizational conditions that allow teachers arriving in a new country to be effective. For example, although New Urban High School employs many OTTs, it reaps little measurable gain from the practice. As a transiently oriented school, New Urban expects high teacher turnover, underinvests in teacher development, and has seen little growth in student achievement. Assuming teachers are "just passing through" led New Urban to take the position that whether one teacher or a dozen teachers leave, they will "just get more" migrant teachers. The teachers are hired for their subject specialism and little institutional attention is paid to their adjustment to American classrooms, students, communities, and pedagogical practices. They are "better than substitutes" who lack subject specialism—and at New Urban, that is deemed to be enough.

Transience is not just a measure of relative turnover; it is a state of mind and an orientation to teachers' work. New Urban High School is not a high-turnover school because it hires OTTs. Rather, it hires OTTs because it is a high-turnover school. This is an important distinction.

In the contrasting case of Central High School, the school administration treats its OTTs as transplants. Its students achieve higher than expected student achievement patterns in math exams and the math department head attributes the department's success to its transplanted, stable teaching population—a situation that results, in part, from induction efforts that support teachers in their introduction into American classrooms, involvement with the local community, and adjustment to American urban students. These transplanted teachers are supported in order to add cultural awareness and culturally appropriate relational skills to their substantial subject matter knowledge. However, the transplant orientation did more than contribute to teacher retention. At Central High, it built a solid and stable teacher population that was better positioned to increase student achievement.

Most overseas trained Filipino teachers indicate a desire for transplant. They aspire to stay and, in working toward this goal, they contribute more time and energy to their students and schools than teachers who adapt to or embrace the short-term visas. They are willing and able to put in the time and energy it takes to adjust to the new teaching context, and they become highly qualified and effective teachers academically, relationally, and culturally. Overseas trained teachers who receive the support of a transplant-oriented work environment are much more likely to make a successful transition.

An effective approach could be to treat all OTTs, even those on short-term visas, like transplant teachers. A New Urban that inducts and supports its OTTs as Central does might see very different student results. New teacher induction research supports this premise, showing that brand new teachers with induction see higher test score results with their students than new teachers without that same developmental support. Overseas trained teachers need different sorts of induction, certainly, yet they also need induction to be successful teachers.[1] With specialized induction support, it may be that OTTs can be effective sooner and contribute more to student learning in high-poverty U.S. schools.

As it now stands, transnational teacher migration into the United States fails to serve most of its participants well. Most OTTs interviewed for this book were not savvy adapters, nor did they embrace their short-term visas. Most schools encountered had transient orientations, and OTTs taught more American students in transiently oriented schools than in transplant schools. Of the Filipino teachers interviewed, only three had plans to maximize the benefits of the short-term visa, while the other thirty saw themselves as coming to "the land of milk and honey."[2] These teachers do not have tangible plans to maximize their fleeting time in the United States. Instead, they hope that some undefined "something" will enable them to stay. They work hard, accept any post offered, and tolerate working conditions that many other teachers would reject. Although these teachers are the most eager to be transplanted into the system, they are, ironically, concentrated in the transient schools where they are the least likely to be retained as teachers. They serve the students most in need of highly qualified and effective teachers, the students most in need of a stable teacher workforce—and, in fact, the students least likely to get either.

The examples of Central and New Urban highlight the ways that schools contribute to transnational teacher failure and success. When OTTs fail to be effective with students, when they fail to make the transition to a new culture and community, then attention must be paid to the context of their work. Schools can engender success or failure, and the framing and reception of the teachers they choose to employ is an essential part of everyone's success.

American Public Schools

Currently, most U.S. schools drawing on the overseas market are organized for high turnover, short-term, subject specialist teachers. Assuming and getting transience, the schools minimize investment in teachers, and undervalue the importance of cultural adjustment, community connection, student relationships, and induction. The focus is on the subject knowledge that specialist teachers can bring to students, while neglecting the importance of relationships and cultures in effectively relaying that knowledge. Narrowing teachers' work down to such a one-dimensional aspect, and treating them as readily interchangeable parts, contributes to the casting of teaching as low-status work.

American urban schools are caught between the pressures of policy mandates on the one hand and the limits of their local capacity to attract the teachers they need on the other. Federal legislation to alter the workforce to require fully qualified teachers do not include the means to achieve those goals. Schools must seek ways to alter their local workforce composition. Districts that have historically struggled to attract and retain teachers are not well positioned to respond to teacher quality requirements. Increased pay, improved working conditions, and enhanced professional status could all help the schools to attract well-qualified teachers. These changes, however, are costly and time consuming to implement. The very schools that need these resources the most are the least likely to have them.

Overseas trained teachers present one, of many, cost-effective supply-side solutions for urban high-poverty school districts. Internship programs like Teach For America and newly credentialed or credentialing teachers are other low-cost supply-side options. The schools that seek short-term overseas teacher labor tend to be the same schools that draw heavily on these other short-term labor market solutions. Collectively, these supply sources enable "hard-to-staff" schools to meet the highly qualified teaching requirements. It does not, however, address the root causes of the staffing challenges, it does not make the schools or the work more attractive to teachers, and it does not ensure a stable and sustainable teaching population at the school level.

When high-poverty American urban schools look to the global market to meet their staffing challenges, they are looking for supply-side rather than demand-side solutions. Overseas trained teachers are one of many of the supply sources that these districts can draw on to meet the demands for qualified teachers in the short term. In the long term, however, this practice does nothing to address the conditions that made these schools hard-to-staff in the first place.

It is possible to retain OTTs, to aid in their adjustment to American classrooms and students, and to increase their effectiveness as teachers. It is possible for OTTs to add important value to the education of American students living in low-income urban environments. Central High School's success indicates that it is possible for New Urban High School and other schools to enjoy the same benefits.

The Teaching Profession

Transnational teacher migration creates a labor dynamic that is unfamiliar in the United States and, in many ways, on a global level. The professional chutes and ladders of teacher migration represent a career contour that is very different from the one that is characteristic of American teachers. It creates financial and professional incentives to work in America's most high-poverty schools and alters both their motivations to teach and their interests in which subject to teach. It expands the teacher labor market from a local to a global frame with economics determining distribution.

American teachers do not generally view teaching at high-poverty urban schools as professionally rewarding. There are few extrinsic advantages to teaching in more challenging schools or working with more challenging students. Many teachers seek to experience the intrinsic rewards of a job well done, an awareness of making a difference in their students' lives, and a desire to contribute to social change; however, working in high-poverty urban schools typically does not come with higher pay or professional recognition, and the working conditions in these schools are often inferior to those at higher-status schools. For OTTs from developing countries, however, the economic and professional rewards are tangible and abundant. Teaching in high-poverty schools in the United States becomes an opportunity to migrate to dramatically higher professional salaries and to gain status and prestige in their home countries. It creates unprecedented extrinsic rewards to teaching.

When Filipino teachers migrate to U.S. schools, they experience a pay increase of more than thirteen times their annual salary. With the home salary of the Filipino teachers averaging $364 dollars monthly and a U.S.

salary averaging over $4,900 monthly, the economic incentives are clear. Expressed in annual terms, that is $4,400 versus $59,400.[3] It has become the case that many teachers around the world are paid at a rate that cannot comfortably sustain them in the economy in which they live. Transnational teacher migration offers one solution to that conundrum. It keeps the local teacher pay scale relatively low by attracting a supply of teachers whose living expenses are in a different economy, thus creating a new incentive to teach in the most needy schools of receiving countries.

Transnational teacher migration shifts the landscape of the teaching profession. It creates extrinsic motivations of dramatically increased pay and status opportunities that allow and affect the distribution of teachers. Migration itself becomes a motivation to teach. Recall that fifteen of the nineteen Filipino special education teachers interviewed in this study entered special education in order to migrate as teachers to the United States.

All of the Filipino teachers interviewed gave economics as a primary motivation for migration. As the South Africa to England literature suggests, this pattern exists in other developing to industrialized nation migrations. Charlie, the South African teacher unhappy with the behavior of his London students, endures the discomfort and permits their disrespectful manners because he values the economic gain. "You turn, put your hands in your pockets and think pounds," he says. However, these economic gains come with psychic costs.

If nothing else, transnational teacher migration draws participants into the profession and into areas—both geographic and pedagogical—that vary from the historical profile of why and where people teach. They introduce a new set of incentives, motivations, and commitments to and from teaching. It shifts the teacher labor market from a local to a global frame and calls on us all to reconsider the contours of the profession.

Role of Industrialized Nations in Teacher Migration

In the United States—and in other industrialized nations as well—OTTs are small in overall numbers, but high in both policy significance and their tangible impact on the schools where they teach and students with whom they work. They offer the potential for improved student outcomes depending on how schools make use of the expanded labor pool.

Industrialized countries serve themselves best by attending to the elements that maximize their own benefits.

But more than that, industrialized countries have an important role to play in the global migration of teachers. They have the power to pull teachers from their homelands, and their economic strength drives the global distribution of teachers. Their orientation to teachers' work and their framing of teachers' reception defines teachers' status in society. Are OTTs elite professionals from their homelands who have been recruited to help the neediest schools of industrialized nations? Are the teachers supported in making the transition to the new culture, school, and student population so they can be as effective as possible? Or, are the OTTs a little "better than substitutes?" Are they left to fend for themselves in an extreme case of sink or swim? Are they merely short-term solutions that can be readily replaced?

The way schools in industrialized countries answer these questions will inform the degree to which teacher migration into industrialized countries is a benefit to those countries. It will also inform the degree to which teachers' work is perceived overall as low-status or high-status work, both locally and globally. The issue of transnational teacher migration is an issue of teachers' work.

The 2011 International Summit on Teaching and the Profession concluded that the highest student achievement and equity patterns are achieved in the countries where teaching is perceived as a high-status occupation. The summit attendees concluded, great systems treat the teaching profession as high-status work, and great systems attract great teachers. Finland is rated as having among the highest national student achievement scores and the greatest degree of student equity in achievement patterns. They also had 6,000 applicants in 2010 for 600 teaching jobs. People want to become teachers in Finland—an option that offers them career prospects, autonomy in the classroom, and responsibilities as professionals for leadership and reform.[4] They have high status as professionals.

How industrialized countries navigate the OTT labor market says much about their attitude toward the status of teachers. Transnational teachers can be framed as low-status guest workers hired to do the work that domestic teachers will not; or transnational teachers can be integrated as an important and valuable source of professional labor. These two framings constitute distinctly different realities for individual teachers, for the experience of schools, and for the implications for the teaching profession.

In Sum: Organizing for the Transnational Teacher

This is a book about the movements of teachers between nations: the scope, patterns, reasons, and the relative success of those movements. At the same time, it is also about what it means to be a teacher today—and about what it will mean to be a teacher tomorrow.

The migration of OTTs to industrialized countries is a symptom, rather than a cause, of an orientation that frames teachers' work as narrowly subject specialist, the teacher workforce as high-turnover, and teachers themselves as readily interchangeable low-status workers.

Industrialized countries have an important role to play in the transnational teacher labor market. They can implement teacher-sourcing practices and policies that treat teachers with respect, provide targeted reception and training, frame the teaching profession as high-status work, and achieve the student results they seek.

Schools in industrialized nations get the transnational teachers for whom they organize. In doing so, a global conception of teachers' work is being forged and a conception of the transnational teacher is emerging. Ultimately, we get the teachers for whom we organize. As we move forward, a key question must be answered: For what type of teacher shall we organize?

As I finish this book, the issues in the teacher labor market are markedly different than when I started the research. School districts are laying off teachers rather than seeking them. Budget crises, coupled with declining enrollments in some areas, are creating a teacher labor surplus and overseas trained teachers are not needed in the same numbers, if at all. This might lead some to conclude that transnational teacher migration is over, that overseas trained teachers are no longer part of the U.S. labor market and that we need not concern ourselves with the details of those migrations. This conclusion would be inaccurate.

Transnational teacher migration is here to stay. The current ebb and flow into the United States is just another aspect of the teacher migration—especially one with a transient orientation to teacher labor. Industrialized countries can turn the tap on when they need more teachers and turn it off when that need diminishes. The existence of the supply, however, remains and can be tapped again at any time.

This ebb is just another part of the transnational teacher labor migration process. Being able to send teachers home is part of the appeal of the global market. Overseas trained teachers can and do join unions, participate in collective bargaining, sign employment contracts, and earn tenure. None of these structures or labor agreements protect their employment when they lose their work visa. All an employer needs to do is elect not to renew the work visa of an OTT and the employment comes to an end; collective bargaining is no help, the contract is invalidated, and the tenure irrelevant. The OTT loses the legal right to remain in the country and must bear the costs of return travel while having no recourse to unemployment in the United States.

Nonrenewal of teacher work visas routinely occurs in U.S. school districts. In some cases, these districts have elected to adopt nonrenewal policies on all OTT visas—effectively discontinuing the employment of every transnational teacher in its employment as their current work visas expire. Districts can discontinue the visas of selected individuals without following union and legal due process employment termination procedures. In this event, teachers are told that their visa, but not their employment, has been discontinued. Teachers who are able to secure a work visa in another manner can therefore retain their positions. Presenting this as an option is, of course, disingenuous as work visas are tied to employers and an alternative visa is nearly impossible to come by (a notable example being a visa gained through marriage to an American citizen).

The global market provides a low-cost source of temporary teacher labor that can be drawn on in times of need and sent back with little direct fiscal cost to schools or the host society. The market can ebb and flow—and ebb and flow it does. There are costs though, as detailed in this book: costs to teacher quality, student achievement, and the teaching profession. These are costs that can be mitigated through policy changes that regulate transnational teacher migration, expand definitions of teacher quality, enhance school success, and protect the rights of all teacher workers regardless of nation of origin.

There are ways to draw on the transnational teacher labor market that can benefit the students and schools of industrialized nations. There are ways that industrialized nations can maximize their own benefits while minimizing the costs to developing countries, migrant teachers, and the teaching profession. New Urban High School is a warning of the ways we can waste and exploit the opportunities of globalization. Central High School offers an example of how to maximize the opportunity of a mobile workforce. Central High School's policies and practices can be realized at other such schools—even at schools such as New Urban High School—through policy changes that can reduce teacher transience, increase the likelihood of teacher transplant, improve educational equity, and expand the overall quality and effectiveness of the teacher workforce.

There are many areas of educational policy that merit refinement. For example, the current No Child Left Behind definition of highly qualified teachers could be expanded to include elements beyond subject expertise. Defining teacher quality as also encompassing pedagogical practice, cultural relevancy, and effective aspects of teachers' work has the potential to shift hiring orientations and employment practices to the benefit of student learning. In addition, creating metrics to assess schools on collective capacity—for example, on school level faculty turnover rates and overall distribution of teacher seniority—could clearly identify what it means to be a well-qualified school rather than simply a school staffed by qualified teachers. According to current policy definitions, a school staffed with all qualified teachers in their first few years of teaching and a faculty turnover rate of 75 percent annually is as well qualified as a school with an even distribution of qualified teachers from the first through twenty-fifth year of teaching and a 10 percent annual faculty turnover rate. The examples of New Urban High and Central High suggest this is not the case and attending to expanding the framing of teacher and school quality is an important policy consideration.

The debates about teacher quality and school capacity are, however, already well underway, and although teacher migration contributes to that discussion it is only one of many elements to be considered. Much more central to the phenomena of teacher migration, and much less in the limelight, is the need for an occupation-specific visa. I am going to focus my attention here on the intersection of education and immigration policy to suggest the need for a teacher-specific visa.

A Teacher Visa

Current labor immigration policies and practices do not maximize the possible benefits of transnational teacher migration into the United States. This situation could be vastly improved through the creation of a teacher visa tailored to the unique needs of the public sector, the schools, and the teaching profession.

The current U.S. visa options available to employ overseas trained teachers are insufficient. Neither the H1B nor the J-1 visa is working well for anyone—except perhaps the for-profit recruitment agencies that generate income through the high turnover of "guest worker" teachers. If public schools are to draw productively on the overseas teacher labor market then they need a visa that fits their employment policies and needs. The teachers themselves deserve to be treated ethically and responsibly and the teaching profession will benefit from a visa process that treats them as high-status global professionals, not low-status migrant workers. This in turn will allow schools, students, and society to benefit from a higher-status teaching profession as it attracts, retains, and sustains better quality teaching and thereby improves student achievement.

Restrictions governing visa start dates and the lottery conditions of visa assignment are poorly aligned with the schedule and hiring needs of school districts. The short-term nature of the visas negatively influences renewal and emigration options, thereby preventing the retention of well-qualified and effective teachers. This in turn reduces school investment in OTTs as money spent on teachers "just passing through" can be seen as money wasted. Furthermore, public school employers are out of their depth navigating the immigration and visa world. It is not part of their expertise or administrative preparation, and they have run afoul of the policies to the detriment of their schools.

The financial and structural penalties set up to punish employers for labor visa violations are also inappropriate for public school employers. Consider the case of Prince George's County Public School District (PGCPS), in Maryland. Conditions of the H1B visa include the requirements that employers bear the visa costs to ensure that OTTs are compensated at a level equal to their domestic colleagues and that American workers are not disadvantaged in hiring decisions. In PGCPS, however, teachers holding H1B visa were required to pay for their own fees. The school district was charged, found in violation of the terms, fined over $100,000 in civil penalties, and banned for two years from applying for new H1B visas, submitting extensions to existing visas, or processing applications for permanent residency. Unlike a private employer, however, this fine did not come out of the profit margin of a corporation; it came instead out of the public funds of an underresourced school district struggling to meet the needs of a low-income urban student population—students who were then also faced with the abrupt exit of established teachers.[1]

The Limits of Existing Visas

The H1B and J-1 visas are insufficient in both similar and different ways. Neither visa is transparent—meaning neither allows an easy identification and count of the number and employment location of OTTs in the United States. Consequently, it is not possible to readily track the annual flows or cumulative populations of OTTs. Beyond that, however, each visa has its merits and limitations in facilitating effective transnational teacher migration.

The overseas trained Filipino teachers prefer H1B visas for several reasons: the costs are assigned to the employer and the H1B allows for up to six years of employment, does not have a repatriation clause, and offers the possibility of emigration. Teachers have more rights and opportunities on an H1B visa, which acknowledges that teachers are there because of a labor shortage and does not force them to go through the motions of a sham cultural exchange. The H1B does not require or even presume permanent emigration, but it does allow teachers and employers to pursue it. And even if teachers return to their home countries at the end of the six years, both they and the schools have had six consecutive years of stable employment.

Because the H1B's lottery selection process creates uncertainty of result, both teachers and school districts alike find this problematic. Many teachers languish in their home country year after year waiting for a successful visa lottery result. And for districts, the H1B lottery timing and inherent uncertainty does not permit for timely employment practices. School districts ideally interview and hire in the spring months for the following academic year. The April lottery date is early for them to have already identified the prospective teacher and completed the lottery paperwork. And the uncertainty of securing a visa through the lottery creates little incentive to get organized earlier in the process. It is difficult to make real plans based on a lottery. Furthermore, the October 1 visa start date is problematic for many schools. Most K–12 academic years begin in late August or early September. An October H1B visa start date leaves classrooms without teachers at the start of the year.

School districts are also troubled by the H1B application process and costs. The H1B requires that employers first certify the open positions as labor shortage areas as defined by Congress and verified by the U.S. Department of Labor. That the costs of the H1B visa are paid by the employer is often felt to be problematic by school districts as it increases the cost of employing an overseas trained teacher. This may have policy benefits—such as increasing the likelihood of local hiring—but it also further discourages districts from using the H1B when other visas are possible. The H1B is, at least, a labor shortage visa that acknowledges a labor market need and permits a three- to six-year solution via an overseas employment visa with the possibility of emigration. Employers may sponsor employees on an H1B for permanent residency (aka a green card). The residency may not be granted, but they may seek it.

In contrast, the J-1 visa circumvents the timing problems, lottery uncertainty, and employer costs related to the H1B. School employers appear to prefer J-1 visas as an initial teacher entry visa because they offer the timing flexibility needed by schools as they may begin at any time and are not numerically controlled by Congress. They are issued for a year and are renewable twice for a possible total of three years. Employers are not required to pay visa-related costs.

J-1 visas, however, are not intended as labor shortage visas. They are short-term cultural exchange visas that presume and require repatriation. None of the school or district employers included in this research sought out the migrant teachers for cultural exchange. They simply needed teachers to fill a perceived labor shortage. This contradiction between visa purpose and employer practice creates awkward working conditions for teachers—including an annual concern about visa renewal. It also makes it difficult to retain successful overseas teachers beyond the three years.

That only authorized agencies can sponsor a J-1 visa can be both a resource and a possible problem for teachers. Keeping the visa separate from the employer allows a teacher to change schools or districts without losing the visa. It also gives the sponsoring agency a great deal of power—power that can be used to protect and support teachers but also can be used to exploit and control them. For example, the California Department of Education sponsored the J-1 visas of many of the Spanish teachers we interviewed, providing them with information about issues such as family visas and support in the event of a necessary employer change. However, the private company that sponsored many of the Filipino teachers' visas operated very differently, imposing additional limitations on the teachers. Most notable was the company's policy that denied the teachers visas for their dependent spouses and children. Instead the agency required teachers to earn the privilege of family reunification through a successful one-year performance review and visa renewal.

Employment Practices

Both J-1 and H1B visas are incompatible with the union contracts and tenure practices of many public schools. Union contracts typically ensure that teachers can earn security of employment through tenure after a predetermined time period and performance review. Contracts may also specify that dismissals after tenure follow a seniority pattern in layoffs and that a due process be practiced in performance terminations. These contracts do not, however, have any power over work visas. In practice this means an OTT can earn tenure and work under a contract but lose employment through visa loss. This can and does happen.

Consider the case of Evelyn Francisco, an OTT who had taught in California's Oakland School District for nine years when that school district elected to not renew her visa. A Filipino teacher recruited by the district from her home country, she had tenure, a contract, and nine years seniority as a math teacher at Oakland Technical High School. The district had brought her over on a J-1 visa in 2001 and then sponsored her for an H1B visa in 2004 and an H1B renewal and permanent residency application in 2007. In 2010 her H1B was about to expire and the U.S. government had not yet processed her permanent residency application. She approached the district to sign off on an administrative extension to the H1B and they refused, citing a change in the labor market making the reliance on OTTs no longer necessary.

Ms. Francisco filed suit, asserting that her job contract guaranteed her tenure and seniority within the Oakland School District and that the district had terminated her employment without due process. In response, the district asserted that it had not terminated her employment and that her tenure and seniority were secure if she could produce another work visa. The district also attempted to remove the case to federal court. The attempt failed when the district court concluded it lacked jurisdiction over the case, because no federal law was implicated. Although the case deals with immigration issues, there was no claim that any immigration law had been violated. After remand to the state trial court, the state judge ruled in favor of the Oakland School District, finding there was no contractual obligation for the employer to sponsor this work visa. Ms. Francisco thus lost her visa and her employment and had to return to the Philippines without recourse or support after nine years of teaching in the same secondary school.

The decision against Evelyn Francisco underscores the contingent labor status of migrant teachers in U.S. schools and the conflicted position of public school employers in relation to them. The teachers are recruited to meet vital labor market needs in high-poverty urban communities. Their visas are intended to be short term. Once in schools, however, they move into an employment structure designed to reward longevity with security of employment. The contradictory message sent by these competing orientations—short-term visas with permanent employment status—is problematic. It misleads the teachers, allows the schools to circumvent labor contracts, and creates a secondary class of teachers in employment practices. The visa terms and labor contracts are clearly out of alignment. Either migrant teachers should not be allowed to earn tenure and seniority—an open and transparent acknowledgement of their short-term and contingent status—or visas must account for the possibility of transition to permanent employment status.[2]

The visas currently available to sponsor migrant teachers are inadequate and inappropriate to the needs of schools and teachers. A specialized visa is needed for the teaching profession.

Precedent for a Teacher Visa

A specialized teacher visa is needed as much to protect the interests of students and American teacher supply, as it is to ensure the well-being of migrant teachers. Students perform better when their schools have stable populations of qualified teachers. American teacher supply will be less impacted if the costs and conditions of employing OTTs are not dramatically lower than domestically sourced teachers. Overseas trained teachers can be an important resource and asset to American schools. The contributions they can make, however, are best reaped through cultivating a stable transplanted migrant teacher program rather than the transience currently enacted through short-term visas and a high-turnover orientation.

There is a precedent for an occupation-specific visa in the nursing profession. Though it lapsed in 2009, for many years the H1C served as a visa for registered nurses working in health professional shortage areas as defined by the U.S. Department of Labor. This visa detailed the qualifications of nurse applicants and defined the possible locations and terms of employment. Under the H1C, nurses were only employed in U.S. Department of Labor–defined healthcare shortage areas at hospitals with at least 190 acute care beds and a Medicaid service population of at least 28 percent. The visa did not allow extensions beyond three years nor did it permit immigration. The visa did, however, make the terms and purpose of employment very clear. Foreign nurses were granted short-term visas to work in health-care facilities that served a low-income population. They could stay for three years and no longer.[3]

Similar clarity, though not necessarily identical terms, is needed for the teacher visa. While some elements of the visa would best be worked out in a national conversation of needs, priorities, and preferences, some aspects are already clearly based on the poor utility of the H1B and J-1 visas. A teacher visa to mitigate labor shortages ought to be a labor shortage visa, not a cultural exchange visa. It should be timed to fit the academic school year and the hiring practices of public schools. Information about where OTTs are employed and in what capacity ought to be very easily discerned, tracked, and made publicly available. A teacher-specific visa would enable easy identification of OTT numbers and patterns.

Furthermore, the findings of this research also argue for a visa that permits the retention, through emigration, of effective and qualified teachers. High teacher turnover is not beneficial for schools or students. Stability of employment for well-qualified and successful teachers is a boon to understaffed schools. Creating a global revolving door of guest worker teachers in and out of low-income schools and back and forth between nations grossly diminishes the possible net gains of teacher labor migration. The United States could benefit by retaining talented teachers. Creating clear avenues for schools to retain effective teachers is just good sense. Sending effective and established teachers away is counterproductive to meeting the achievement and equity goals of public education.

Of course, not all OTTs will transition successfully to teaching in American schools, and school demand for OTTs will not remain constant. In cases where teacher employment is terminated prematurely (i.e., before the end of contracted and visa-permitted employment), provision should be made for these teachers' early return. In instances where unemployment would be paid, OTTs should receive a visa/contract termination fee. This will help ensure equitable treatment of all teachers. It will bring contract agreements and visa conditions into better alignment. It will also work to counter the situation where migrant teacher labor is more contingent and by extension more flexible and perhaps preferable, to that of domestic teachers.

Using visas as an employment management tool creates differences between the terms of employment for what are quickly becoming two classes of public schools teachers. While the United States may want to structure work visas so as to protect the employment opportunities of Americans, the steps best taken to do so may not be as simple as minimizing the job opportunities and securities of foreign teachers. When work becomes "guest work" and workers have few rights or recourse to due process, that work becomes lower status and the contingent workers more desirable to employers. The existence of a contingent teacher supply drives down the working conditions and respect for all teachers. A properly structured teacher visa can minimize this downside of teacher migration by creating safeguards to protect the rights of OTTs and by extension the rights and status of all teachers.

Again, the details of a teacher visa need to be worked out in conversation with more stakeholders—however, the need for a teacher visa is evident. A well-structured teacher visa can make the importing of teachers into U.S. schools work better for the schools themselves, has the potential to improve student educational experience and outcomes, and can do much to protect the teaching profession in the United States and elsewhere. Current visa options are ill-suited to the teaching profession and create problems that a dedicated occupational visa could address. The United States is importing teachers. Now we need to build the systems to do it responsibly and effectively.

The research for this book began as an abiding curiosity into a set of questions about teacher migration. I wanted to know the extent of international teacher migration, the function it plays in teacher labor markets, the experience of teachers, schools and students—and also, of course, the implications for the teaching profession. I felt very much like a sleuth as I sought ways to answer those questions as fully as I could with each piece of the puzzle leading to a new question and the search for yet more answers.

The data collection sequence reflects this investigation. An exploratory phase gave rise to a scope and pattern analysis of established large-scale data sets. This in turn led to a multipronged qualitative inquiry of teacher, school, and school district experience. Collectively, this generated multiple sources and types of data. Analysis occurred both within and across these data sets and types to piece together a full and complex picture of transnational teacher migration.

To claim that this data collection pathway was clearly marked and the route planned in advance of the research journey would be disingenuous. The design was emergent. Each step of the path led to signposts that indicated the next move. I employed a phenomenological situated analysis of transnational teacher migration into the United States with particular attention paid to California as a receiving state, Filipino teachers as a teacher supply, and urban schools as a site of employment. The design was emergent and the foci determined during data collection and analysis. For example, California was selected as a focal state both because it was one of the major seekers of overseas trained teacher labor certification and because a data source for considering supply sources was identified. Filipino teachers were a focus in the book because the

California data revealed them to be the most significant source of overseas trained teachers.

Inspired by a sense that there was something as yet unseen and undocumented in the teacher workforce patterns I was encountering, I felt my way forward in exploring the topic and mapping the terrain. The data collection took place in three distinct phases. In an initial exploratory phase, I discovered the phenomenon of OTT migration and sought out existing research and reports on the subject. The clear lack of information on the extent of teacher migrations led to the stage two investigation of scope and pattern. This stage emphasized the identification and statistical analyses of large-scale data sets that allowed determinations as to how many OTTs were sought by U.S. schools, where they were teaching, and their nations of origin. Stage three, a qualitative and ethnographic data stage, attended to the experience of teachers and schools in context. It included interviews with fifty OTTs employed in California public schools, case studies of three California high schools where these teachers work, interviews with human resource directors at the top employing school districts, and observations gathered by following a newly arrived cohort of OTTs through their orientation and first year in U.S. schools. Data analysis was ongoing and reiterative within and across data sets.

Finding and Refining the Research Questions

As touched upon in the preface, I came to the topic of transnational teacher migration through a series of unexpected professional encounters.

I was an overseas trained teacher long before I knew to call it such. In the early 1990s, I was a freshly minted secondary school English teacher in Massachusetts. Or rather I wanted to be a teacher. I was well prepared to teach with a bachelor's degree, with honors, in English literature, a master's degree in curriculum and instruction, and a state teaching certificate. It was, however, a time of budget shortfalls and teacher layoffs and I could not find a full-time permanent post. Familiar with England from my time there as an undergraduate exchange student and through continued personal contacts, I knew that country to be experiencing a severe teacher shortage. I sought and secured an English teaching post at a comprehensive secondary school just north of London.

My experience was more like the teachers from Spain than the Filipino teachers. I was young, I had no dependents or debts, and I went to

England seeking teaching work and adventure. I did not leave the United States because I was unable to support myself. And although my visa process was complicated and expensive (including an unexpected necessary trip back to the United States two months after my arrival in England to secure the visa); my pay was abysmally poor (the school would not recognize my American master's degree in determining my pay); my talents were routinely in question (one school turned down my employment application for not being a native "English" speaker; colleagues at my school of employment discouraged me from teaching American literature; and my students' parents fretted I might ruin their children's spelling), I never felt trapped or stuck. I knew I could return to the United States at any time. I had a tremendously interesting experience and moved from there to California and a new adventure.

More than a decade later I returned to England as an Atlantic Public Policy Fellow to look at the ways England was working to improve its teacher workforce stability. Although England was making changes to cultivate and sustain its domestic teacher supply (including a nationwide marketing campaign to recruit teachers as well as taking steps to reduce teacher working time), it had also vastly accelerated its overseas hiring. I discovered this by chance while visiting London schools heavily staffed with South African teachers. Although I had once come to England seeking employment, now the English schools actively recruited from other countries.

Once again I left England for California—this time for a faculty appointment at the University of California. In my first year back, I discovered the recruitment of overseas teachers was also practiced by public schools in California. The parallel practice in England and California—pulling as they were respectively from South Africa and the Philippines—led me to posit there was something happening that merited exploration.

There appeared to be a globalization of teacher labor markets that needed closer study and illumination. In 2004, I began to look for research and publications on the topic. I found little that even described the phenomenon, let alone analyzed or critiqued it. There were a few news reports and the white paper that came out of the Commonwealth Secretariat meeting in Scotland, but nothing that seriously captured either the scope of hiring overseas or the patterns of teacher migration. Nothing that provided a sense of the degree to which hiring overseas might be an interesting but rare and isolated local solution or a larger-scale shift in hiring practices, job search orientations, and labor markets. No one had yet to document the scope and pattern of transnational teacher migration.

Research on the teaching profession, teachers' working lives, and labor markets have traditionally been nationally bound or even, in places like the United States, focused on smaller areas at the state level. Tracking teacher migration patterns internationally sits outside of conventional educational data collection frames and concerns—for example, state and national teacher quality reporting do not attend to teachers' country of origin, and years of teaching experience is chronicled but not work visa status or the nation in which professional preparation or teaching experience was gained. The teacher research field was not well positioned to consider questions about international movements and, as a scholar in that field, neither was I. Studying this phenomenon ultimately required that I construct a data set in order to answer questions previously unasked in teacher workforce research and data collection.

In an effort to understand the scale of teacher migration, I undertook many hours of Internet and library searches, a broad set of far-ranging conversations, and a multitude of forays into schools, district offices, and government agencies. In the end, I was able to document the scope and pattern of OTTs in the United States and to take a closer look at California through several years of data collection and a driving determination to piece together the story of teacher migration.

I identified a way to map the scope and pattern of OTT demand in the United States by using the publicly available U.S. Department of Labor's database on Labor Condition Applications (LCAs) made by employers seeking to hire foreign nationals under the congressionally regulated H1B labor shortage visas. Labor market visas and immigration policy were new areas for me and required me to navigate new domains. It was well worth the effort. The LCA data made it possible to identify patterns of demand for OTTs by year, geography, and employer. It made the trend visible.

Access to a previously unexamined data set that tracked the country of professional preparation of newly credentialed teachers in California was also essential to scope and pattern analysis. The California Commission on Teacher Credentialing had, for many years, collected information on the country of education and professional preparation of OTTs. That the commission had neither analyzed these data nor made them public was due to a general lack of public and policy interest in the topic as well as inadequate staff resources. The agency graciously made these data available to me in exchange for my willingness to share analysis and findings with the commission.

In addition, I sought out and interviewed several OTTs. Although these early interviews are not part of the final data set used in the analysis for this book, they were essential in helping to refine my research questions and hone my understanding of teacher migration. These interviews informed my decision to pursue a multilevel qualitative inquiry at the teacher, school, and district level.

Collectively, the U.S. Labor Condition Application data, the California teacher credentialing data, and the early interviews allowed me to craft a preliminary design plan. Access to the LCA and state credential data would allow a national scope and pattern analysis with a deeper look into California patterns. Based on these findings, I would then craft the next steps of inquiry. I knew I wanted to better understand teachers— their experiences of migration as well as schools' experiences of migrant teachers. The preliminary interview data highlighted the need for greater and deeper qualitative inquiry, the details of which I would work out after the national and state pattern analysis.

Getting at Scope and Pattern

This stage of research was driven by questions regarding the scope and pattern of overseas trained teachers. How many OTTs are there in the United States? Which regions and school employers seek to hire them? How have the numbers changed over time? What subject areas are sought? From which countries are teachers recruited? And where do they teach in the United States?

Answering these questions was only possible through the construction of a new data set that combined the U.S. Department of Labor's LCA data and data on OTTs gathered by the California Commission on Teacher Credentialing. Bringing these two data sets together was time-consuming and complicated. In addition to needing to clean each data set separately (i.e., removing duplicates and deleting incomplete entries), other steps were required to make the parallel analysis of them productive. For example, each defined the start and end date of a year differently and juxtaposing these data required substantial recoding to make them compatible. The result was a new and unique data set that permitted scope and pattern analysis.

This new employment and credential data set was supplemented by other national and state data sets that contextualize the findings and allow more thorough representation of the patterns. For example, useful information was provided through California's Basic Educational Data System's statistical information on students, schools, and teachers collected annually and made publicly available via the state's Ed-Data website.[1]

Labor Condition Application Data

National scope and pattern of OTT employment is currently best approximated with labor visa data. The U.S. Department of Labor (USDOL) is the arbiter of labor shortage criteria as defined by Congress. Employers seeking to hire foreign nationals on H1B labor shortage visas must first seek authorization to hire in a shortage area through the USDOL Labor Condition Application (LCA) process. These applications and the USDOL decisions on them have been made publicly available since 2002. These data include full employer details, job title, and salary range.

The estimates of employment patterns for OTTs in this book are based on a detailed analysis of the LCA database. Labor certification is necessary for an H1B hire—therefore seeking an LCA is an indication that an employer seeks to hire foreign nationals. It does not guarantee success with the H1B hire and in that way LCAs might overestimate OTT employment with H1B visas. However, given that other visa types such as the J-1 are not captured in these numbers, it seems likely that the J-1 visas not included in these estimates counter any overestimation made by relying on LCA data.

To make the USDOL data set useful required a lengthy process of cleaning and recoding the data. Five steps were involved.

Step 1: The USDOL made the 2002–2008 LCA data available on their website. The data, however, are offered there by submission type (fax or electronic) and by year. This step required that we download all of the files by year and by submission type and merge them into one file for 2002–2008.

Step 2: The LCA data include all employment positions and employers that seek to employ foreign nationals with an H1B visa. A series of culls were required to create a database on just K–12 school employment. First, all education posts were identified using the DOL codes 91–99 roughly corresponding with the nonuniversity education field. These codes are broad, however, and include anything from preschool through higher education and also encompass foreign language centers and even martial arts instructors at fitness centers. Hand-sorting through the data set honed in on strictly K–12 schools, including charter schools, private schools, and employment agencies that serve public schools (employer type codes included P for public school or district, C for public charter school, A for agency, and R for private school). Every precaution was taken to ensure that only employers of K–12 schoolteachers were counted, including web searches for employer details and even phone calls. When in doubt—i.e., when it wasn't possible to establish a public school employment agency or charter school status—LCAs were deleted. This may have contributed to an underestimate of charter school and employment agency participation. In the final counts private schools were excluded.

Step 3: Because only certified LCA applications were counted, all denied applications were deleted from the data set. This minimized over-estimation of OTT employment demand as some denied applications were clearly resubmitted and then certified.

Step 4: The application form required a job title but permitted an open-ended response. Consequently job titles varied significantly and could not be counted readily. Learning the relative distribution by school level and subject area required the assignment of new codes line by line based on the job title sought. The following job categories were used:

1. Math
2. Science
3. Language instructors (e.g., Spanish teacher)
4. ESL/bilingual
5. Special education (including speech therapist)
6. Elementary school teacher
7. Secondary school teacher
8. Other/unclassified
9. Administration (principal, director, etc.)

When coding, preference was given to the greatest level of specificity rather than general classification—i.e., a math teacher was coded under math, not secondary school teacher. The general categories were used only in the absence of specifics. Other categories were not included only because no LCAs were made using them. For example, history teachers were not coded as generic secondary school teachers but rather no one indicated "history teacher" as a job title. Each position was coded only once, and coding was done in order, with job code 1 taking precedence over job code 2. For example a bilingual math teacher is coded as 1–math and not as 4–ESL/bilingual education.

Step 5: The counts were based on calendar years and were calculated using the employers' indicated start date for prospective visas and employees rather than on the application date of the LCA.

These data were then used to answer the scope and pattern questions addressed in Chapter 1. Basic descriptive statistics were employed to look at annual LCA numbers between 2002 and 2008 as well as state-by-state patterns, and to identify geographic concentrations within states and nationally. LCA data highlighted the geographic concentrations in certain urban regions and enabled the identification of major school district employers. It was through this LCA data that California school districts were selected for closer study. This additional work is detailed in the qualitative section of this data collection plan.

The maps in Chapter 1 provide a vivid look at the distribution of OTTs in the United States by region and adjusted for population density. These maps were made using the LCA data (cleaned and coded as stated above), employer zip codes determined population details from the 2000 census, and demographic data on the number of students per state is from the National Center for Educational Statistics at the U.S. Department of Education.

Employment agencies provided an added level of challenge in clearly documenting the scope and pattern of OTTs using LCA data. Located in a single geographic location, agencies may place teachers all over the state or anywhere in the country. Some OTTs end up the employees of independent agencies who then contract them out to school districts. In these cases, the agencies, rather than the school districts, are the visa sponsors and the teachers are their employees. Looking at LCA certifications in these instances does little to reveal the actual workplace of teachers.

Georgia is a perfect example of this phenomenon. In September 2009, the American Federation of Teachers reported Georgia was the 2007 top employer of OTTs based on LCA records.[2] A close look at those LCA records indicates that 4,079 of the 4,383 LCAs certified for Georgia employers were sought by just one employment agency. This agency, according to its marketing materials, places teachers in South Carolina, Louisiana, and Florida as well as Georgia. In fact, between 2002 and 2008, this same agency sought 7,616 of the 8,644 total LCAs requested by Georgia employers. There is no public way to know where those teachers are employed. This one agency accounted for more than 80 percent of all LCAs sought for OTTs between 2002 and 2008 in Georgia. Georgia may indeed have been home in 2007 to the largest number of OTTs sought by any U.S. state, but it also may have simply been home to the most prolific OTT employment agency. The LCA data do not allow a clear view of this practice.

Later in the data collection, I discovered a confounding and limiting factor in the use of the data to approximate OTTs in the United States: a heavy employer reliance on J-1 visas as the point of entry visa. J-1s were the primary visa type encountered in the qualitative data collected in California. Employment agencies and school districts favor the J-1 visa over the H1B because it is both easier to obtain and passes fewer costs to the employer. J-1 visa data are, however, not publicly available in the same way as LCA data related to the H1B visa. In this way the OTT numbers estimated with the LCA data are very likely to be an underestimation as they exclude J-1 visas from the count.

California Teacher Credential Data

Although the LCA data answer questions about the demand for OTTs, this information cannot, by its very nature as a preemployment labor certification, address the supply of OTTs. Identifying the national sources of such teachers required another data set.

The California Commission on Teacher Credentialing (CCTC) collects information on country of teacher education preparation in processing new credential applications. This practice began in 1991 and made possible a longitudinal look at the flow and source countries of overseas teachers into California. The commission had not previously published or even analyzed these data as they were primarily collected to facilitate the credentialing process, not to track overseas teacher migration. The CCTC gave me access to the data in exchange for sharing my analysis—which I did in a formal presentation to a public meeting of the commission.

Identifying information, such as names and contact information, was removed by the CCTC prior to sharing the data to ensure teacher privacy.

Only first credential applications were considered in an effort to count each teacher only once. A certain level of missing data thus limits the research. Thirteen percent of all credential application records indicate a foreign teacher education preparation source without naming a specific source country. These records are indicated as "unknown" in the analysis. If attributed to a single source country, this 13 percent would itself constitute a sufficiently high number (987) to represent a leading source of OTTs. The analysis in Chapter 1 is based solely on the records for which there are national sources attributed.

Descriptive statistics were used to analyze the source countries and numbers of OTTs into California. These numbers were also juxtaposed against the overall patterns of teacher credentialing in California to make determinations about the general significance of OTTs in the California teacher labor market and in relationship to other sources of credentialed teachers (i.e., district preparation programs and institutes of higher education outside of California).

Exploring the District, School, and Teacher Experience

Gaining insight into the experiences of overseas trained teachers and the schools and schools districts that employed them required qualitative and ethnographic data collection in the field.

These data were collected over two academic years (2008–2010), took place completely in California and overlapped with one another in context and timing. Access to one large urban school district afforded context for intensive case study research. Three case study schools and thirty teachers shadowed through their first year of U.S. teaching were all in the same large urban school district. The three schools were selected because they were the places of employment of some of the newly arrived teachers. These embedded contexts provided a deeper and more nuanced look into the experience of teachers and schools participating in the labor migrations.

California School District Employers

The Labor Condition Application data analysis revealed twelve school districts to account for 68 percent of all public schools efforts within California to employ OTTs under the H1B visa between 2000 and 2006. These twelve school districts are predominantly urban and high poverty, and they collectively serve more than a million students a year. In order to understand the reasons school districts sought to hire OTTs, interviews with human resource directors were sought in each district.

Eight of the twelve districts participated in interviews. Of the four districts not participating, three declined and in one case we were not able to arrange an appropriate time for the interview. In five of the participating districts, the interviews took place in person; the other three were phone interviews. The in-person interviews were much richer, being recorded and transcribed. The phone interviews were nevertheless informative and worthwhile in that they allowed a further exploration for the districts' rationale and instrumentation of OTT employment and recruitment.

These interviews were analyzed and coded for recurring themes and are the basis for much of the district details shared in Chapter 1. The most consistent messages across these data were (1) that districts were principally seeking and employing OTTs with and through the help of established private employment recruitment agencies; and (2) that districts hired OTTs because of staffing challenges in meeting the No Child Left Behind highly qualified teacher requirements, not for cultural diversity or language needs.

In the primary case study district, the district that housed New Urban and Central, many interviews and observation hours were conducted within the human resource department over the course of a year. This is the district that invited observation of its OTT orientation and placement process, facilitated meetings with OTTs, and permitted the case study research in three of its schools. This district was typical of many of the other districts that sought to employ OTTs. They did so out of a sense of need and urgency to ensure a supply of teachers that met highly qualified teacher subject requirements.

The case research, along with my more casual conversation and interactions with district personnel, indicate a knowledge limitation to supporting migrant teachers. The intent of district human resource personnel was to navigate the recruitment process with integrity toward teachers and schools. At the same time, however, they were operating outside of their knowledge and comfort zone in regard to migration visas and immigration policy. The district office was clear that it was this awareness of their unfamiliarity with the circumstances of teacher labor migration and their desire to do right by the overseas teachers that motivated them to cooperate with this research project. It was their hope that this work would help them and other school districts to better employ and support OTTs.

Delving into the Experiences of Overseas Trained Teachers

With district access came teacher access. In particular, the case study district generously invited me and my research assistant, Alisun Thompson, to observe the orientation of newly arrived OTTs. Alisun and I shadowed twenty-four Filipino teachers and six Spanish teachers beginning with their second day in the country and continuing on through to their two-week district orientation, to their place of residence, to job fairs and school interviews, and into their classroom placements. These teachers became our primary point of departure for a snowball sample of OTTs. The schools that some of them ended up teaching in eventually became our case study schools.

Over the course of the project, we formally interviewed fifty OTTs. Some of the teachers were interviewed just once while others were interviewed multiple times, both formally and informally, in addition to direct observations. The interviews focused on understanding teachers' personal and professional backgrounds, motivations for migration, and experience of migration, as well as their challenges, goals and plans. Across these interviews, both individual and collective stories were identified and explored.

Of the fifty teachers interviewed, thirty-three were from the Philippines, with thirteen of them part of the cohort of twenty-four Filipino teachers newly arrived in 2008. Eight interviewed teachers were from Spain, with six of them also newly arrived within the same 2008 cohort. The remaining teachers interviewed came from India (five), Canada (three), and Brazil (one). Thirty-five of the teachers were women and fifteen were men. The gender split was particularly stark in the Filipino group, with twenty-five female and eight male teachers. In contrast, teachers from Spain included three women and five men.

Fifty was not a predetermined number of interviewees—rather, teacher interviews were stopped at the point of saturation across multiple domains. For example, teachers' pathways to the United States were identified through a saturation analysis as falling into one of three categories: (1) individual, (2) government programs, and (3) recruitment agencies (as described in Chapter 3). A point was reached where the pathway stories repeated themselves across interviews with such frequency that we could almost predict the unfolding of each story during the interview. This was particularly true with the recruitment agency pathway as it was the most frequently encountered and followed an easily identifiable script.

More Indian, Spanish, and Canadian teachers were sought but not located during the data collection phase. The state data numbers indicate Mexico and England are also significant source countries. However, despite concerted effort, we were unable to locate teachers trained in Mexico or England to interview for this study. The research might have been strengthened had we been successful in efforts to identify and interview teachers from more sending countries, especially those excluded or underrepresented by our research methods.

Positionality, in relationship to the OTTs, was sometimes challenging and carefully articulated to them at every opportunity. We emphasized our independence, as university researchers, from their employing school district, but we were also aware that our position was confusing and may, at times, have influenced what they shared with us. In particular, we suspect the teachers often underplayed the negative aspects of their experience—especially in early contact with us. We worked to clarify our position, to be helpful when possible but not to exert undue influence. We strove to stay connected but apart. For example, we stayed out of their decision-making process about school placements and teaching assignments, but offered our support in terms of navigating transportation, resources for information (such as referring them to Craigslist for apartment searches), and sometimes just providing a ride home.

Shadowing Teachers through Orientation and the First Year

In the case study district, thirty teachers (twenty-four Filipino and six Spanish) were shadowed through their arrival into the United States in August 2008, orientation into the district, and first year of teaching in California (2008–2009). All thirty of these teachers taught in the same very large urban school district.

The selection of these particular thirty teachers was a convenience and opportunity sample. The employing school district invited the observation and provided access to the whole process of orientation and job placement. These were the thirty OTTs who were newly employed and arrived in the district.

All but one of the thirty teachers who arrived in the 2008 cohort were on J-1 visas. The Filipino teachers' visas were sponsored by the private employment recruitment agency that placed them with the school district. The Spanish teachers' visas were sponsored by the California Department of Education as part of a formal program with the Spanish government.

Observation of the twenty-four Filipino teachers began two days after they arrived into the United States. Similar observation of the Spanish teachers began a week into their official arrival in the district, though most of them had arrived in the United States much earlier to travel or visit friends. Observation of the whole group, both the merged cohort of Filipino and Spanish teachers and when the cohort was broken out by national origin, continued through the job placement process and into the first week of school. Specific teachers were then selected and followed through the first year of teaching and as an entry point into case studies of their employing schools.

The first week of the orientation took place in the district office and was exclusively for the newly arrived Filipino teachers.[3] At least one research observer was in the orientation meeting at all times. The meeting included presentations by district staff, employees of the recruitment agency, and more seasoned overseas trained Filipino teachers. Topics covered included everything from life logistics, such as housing, banking, and transportation, to professional guidance such as resume preparation, interviewing skills, classroom management, and cultural guidelines for interacting with students and colleagues. It was a veritable smorgasbord of topics selected based on feedback from past experiences and intended to front-load as much transition and support information on a variety of topics as possible.[4] It was in these presentations that many of the employer expectations for the Filipino OTTs were made quite explicit. The Filipino teachers were expected to fill teaching vacancies in the hardest to staff schools in the district; they were not to ever send a student out of a classroom unless they were physically threatened, and they were to return to their home country at the end of their three-year visa. This last point was accentuated in the portion of the orientation covered by the recruitment agency that sponsored their J-1 cultural exchange visas.

An important part of the first week's orientation was the half-day school site visit to schools in session organized by the district. Past cohort experiences had highlighted for the human resource department the importance of increasing the newly arrived teachers' knowledge of American urban schools and classrooms prior to the first day of school. They toured through schools that already employed OTTs, walked through several classrooms, attended an information session with a school administrator, and had an opportunity to speak with some of the Filipino teachers working there.

Although all of the OTTs arrived in the United States with a provisional contract, none of them actually had teaching posts at a school yet. The district practiced a system of centralized screening coupled with local hiring. This meant all of the OTTs had to interview for and secure a teaching post within the district after arriving. Failure to do so would relegate them to either the on-call substitute pool or perhaps a cancelled contract.

Meanwhile, during the time the Filipino teachers were in the district orientation, the Spanish teachers were already out interviewing for teaching posts with schools. A human resource employee drove them in a district van from school to school with some of them interviewed at each school. By the end of that first week all six of them had been offered posts and three of the six had accepted positions. The other three were holding out for positions at schools they deemed more appealing.

During the second week, all of the Spanish and Filipino teachers, together with some American district interns, attended a union-sponsored orientation for new teachers hired through the alternative pathways. Classroom management was addressed again, as were contract details and union structures.

In the middle of that week, the district sponsored a job fair in its main offices. Every cubicle on the human resource floor was assigned to a different school team, folders were posted in the main hallway with job opening information, and prospective teachers popped their resumes into the school folders for which they wanted to be considered. All teachers then gathered in a central area, some perched on an insufficient number of seats and planter box edges while others stood around in anxious clusters. The school year was about to begin and the schools with open positions were mostly schools that had trouble filling their posts. The Filipino and Spanish teachers were mixed in with the district interns along with the traditionally prepared U.S. teachers. A job fair emcee, equipped with a microphone, would call out the names of teachers called for interviews by each school. A district employee would then escort these selected teachers to the school's designated cubicle. Interviews were mostly conducted by assistant principals and took roughly five minutes per teacher. Often at the end of the interview an offer would be extended. None of the teachers from Spain accepted a post that day, though all were offered one. Instead they asked to visit the school before making a decision. All of the Filipino teachers accepted an offered post on the spot.

Not everyone received a post that day. The Spanish teachers delayed the decision. Many of the Filipino teachers were not offered posts and several of them spent the whole day at the fair without being called for a single interview. Those Filipino teachers without posts were even more anxious than before the fair and ready to take absolutely any post offered.

This area of data collection, more than any other in the project, was ethnographic in that it entailed extensive unstructured time spent with the teachers in their schools, homes, and communities. In addition to observing classrooms and orientations, my research assistant and I participated in potluck dinners and karaoke nights, and we attended cultural events and community meetings. We were in the teachers' homes and workspaces. Although informal in nature, these times spent with the teachers were nonetheless important in gaining a more nuanced understanding of the overseas teacher experience.

Case Study Schools

The case study school research was conducted in three secondary schools located in the same district as the orientation cohort of teachers. The schools were selected based on the following criteria:

1. At least one new OTT from the orientation cohort was hired to teach there.
2. Other OTTs were already employed there and had been for at least a year.
3. Case study sites supplied variation in OTT composition, including (a) national origin of teachers employed at the school; and (b) longevity of teacher retention.

The schools all served a similar student population, but that was not a selection criteria. Rather the similarity in school profiles was more the result of the types of schools that employ OTTs. This district, like many urban school districts, brought the OTTs in specifically for their "hard-to-staff schools." The arrival of the teachers just before the school year began helped to ensure they went primarily to schools that struggled with staffing needs.

152

New Urban High, the first school selected, hired several new Filipino OTTs, adding to an already substantial pool of Filipino OTTs on the faculty. One newly hired teacher had been chosen to replace her sister at the school. New Urban was one of the schools that opened itself up to the tours, and it was at the district hiring fair. New Urban did not employ OTTs from countries other than the Philippines.

Central High School was explicitly chosen because it was the only school encountered that had employed OTTs for more than five years. Central employed only Filipino teachers and had hired many in the first 2001 district cohort that were still at the school in 2008. The school was selected in order to capture the experience of teachers who made it beyond the first few years despite time limits in visas.

Ventana High School was included because it hired two of the newly arrived teachers from Spain and one from the Philippines. It also had several more established OTTs, including a substantial pool of second-year teachers from Spain and two Canadian teachers. Ventana High School was explicitly selected for the variation it provided to the school cases. It represented the case of a school that primarily hired teachers from countries other than the Philippines. Both New Urban and Central employed only Filipino teachers while Ventana employed Spanish, Canadian, and Filipino teachers. The same data collection and analysis was carried out at all three schools.

It is important to note that Central and New Urban were not selected as institutional contrast cases. Although the high turnover of New Urban's teacher population and the much more stable teacher workforce at Central would be good grounds for comparable case selection, it was not something that was noted during site selection. Because New Urban had been opened for only five years at that time, its overall lack of long-term teachers seemed understandable. Furthermore, it could not have hired teachers from the 2001 OTT cohort, as it did not yet exist. The contrasts between New Urban and Central, detailed in Chapter 5, became apparent only during data collection and analysis.

Ventana was not included in the Chapter 5 institutional analyses, as it did not offer any additional insight into the dynamics detailed there. It is not referred to by name elsewhere in the book. Analysis revealed Ventana to be a school that employed OTTs migrating "to" rather than "from" something, essentially employing a substantially different teacher population than either New Urban or Central. The research related to

Ventana did, however, help greatly in understanding the different experiences of the teachers from Spain, and this information is used in Chapters 3 and 4 to contextualize the pathways and experiences of a more empowered OTT experience.

At all three schools, case study data collection included three one-day visits during the autumn and again in early January. These visits focused on the new hires, observing them in their classrooms and interviewing them about their experience of the school and the teaching assignment. It also included meetings with the administration to negotiate more complete access. These early visits paved the way for a weeklong visit by two researchers, myself and my research assistant, in February 2009 to observe classrooms of OTTs, to interview OTTs (both new and established) and their American colleagues, and also to conduct interviews with the principal and assistant principals, the department heads, the beginning teacher support coaches/directors, and other school leaders. Follow-up visits at each of the schools and with teachers during the spring came to a total of about two days at each school. State and school district data were analyzed to better contextualize each school's student population, faculty profile, and school achievement patterns.

The purpose of the case study research was threefold: (1) to better understand the experience of OTTs in the context of their schools; (2) to understand the challenges and barriers to success as well as the supports that facilitated teacher adjustment; and (3) to understand the way the local schools framed the teachers and perceived them as members of the faculty and the role they played in the school.

Data Analysis

Data analysis was ongoing throughout the data collection and beyond. It varied by data set in terms of timing and type of data, with earlier stage analysis taking place within sets and later stage analysis occurring across sets. Some of these analyses, like the LCA analysis, occurred earlier in the project and has already been detailed here. Each led to the next round of questions and the employment of additional data collection methods as well as a return to earlier data sets.

An example of how the data sets interrelate is embodied in the trajectory of LCA to teacher credentialing to qualitative data. The LCA data analysis identified high-poverty urban centers as the places where OTTs are concentrated and allowed the identification of the top twelve public

Table A.1 Case study schools' student demographics, 2008–2009

	Number of students	Hispanic (%)	African American (%)	Free/ reduced lunch (%)	English language learners (%)
New Urban					
High School	3,475	92	7.0	69	43
Ventana					
High School	3,377	98	0.3	78	26
Central					
High School	4,461	97	0.2	86	34

school district employers in California. Interviewing human resource directors in these districts built a clear picture of the reasons and rationale for hiring overseas. This in turn sent me to look at the master plans and reports of major OTT employing districts in other states for indications of similar orientations (in particular, that OTTs were seen as a last resort effort to meet labor market teacher needs in the hardest to staff schools).

The California credentialing data indicated that the Philippines was the largest and fastest-growing source for OTTs in that state. That information led me to seek out Filipino teachers in particular for the qualitative interviews on teacher experience—as well as to work to ensure teachers from other source countries were also included. Seeking that concentration and variety is what led to such rich case study school data offering insights into the organizational conditions of OTT work.

As is often the case with complex and deep data collection, moments of insight or surprise would send me back to the data. Thematic coding of the interviews often netted a new insight that necessitated a recoding of earlier interviews. This iterative cycle drew out the findings in empirically driven searches. One prime example of that is in the discovery of the retraining of Filipino teachers in special education in order to migrate to the United States. One of the teachers interviewed was particularly explicit about her decision to retrain as a special education teacher in order to seek employment in the United States. More than half of the special education Filipino teacher interviews had already been coded for motivation, pathway, and experience, yet this one interview pushed me to revisit the previously coded interviews. I thought I had heard some similar references in other interviews, but I had not identified them until this point. As I recoded the interviews, I found references to similar decisions around retraining in every interview—some of them subtle, but some so direct I was a bit chagrined to have missed them the first time through.

I was fortunate to have a research assistant who was nearly as familiar with the data as I was. Alisun Thompson, doctoral student in education at the University of California Santa Cruz, worked closely with me in the teacher interviews, ethnographic field work, and school case studies. She conducted about half of the teacher interviews, was the second researcher in each of the three case study schools and orientation cohort, and also coded each of the interviews. The conversations and debates we had as to appropriate codes, discernment of patterns, and determination of findings were essential to the analysis process. It pushed us both to return to the data repeatedly to seek counter cases and further empirical warrant as we fleshed out the contours of the experiences of OTTs and the schools of their employment.

At its most basic level, this process took the form of our identification of the teacher migration pathways. We had conducted no more than half the interviews before we could discern the recruitment agency pathway (our earlier term for this route was the "hotel ballroom" story as each of the teachers reported taking an abbreviated version of the California teacher test, required for the state credential, with hundreds of other hopeful migrant teachers in a hotel ballroom) as well as the government agency pathway. But the individual pathway was teased out much later in the process as we determined there were some cases that did not fit into the first two emergent categories.

A more nuanced example of these conversations was the ongoing consideration and frequent debate concerning the idea of exploitation versus empowerment of the OTTs. Both Alisun and I sought examples within the data to bolster the argument that the teachers were either exploited by their migration experience and position in the labor market or they were empowered by it. Rather than one of us consistently holding a steadfast position, we tended to switch back and forth—at times both sharing a position and at other times debating the two sides of it. The day we finally recognized that the teachers were in fact both exploited and empowered by their migration experience, that both situations could exist simultaneously, was both a breakthrough in the project analysis and a testimony to the importance of a collaborative analysis process.

The project was long and involved. Data collection took place over years, and documenting and defining a new phenomenon required in-depth analysis of the data—as well as the many benefits of early and frequent public presentation and scrutiny. From the first year of this study, I presented data and preliminary findings at scholarly meetings, casual gatherings of colleagues, and professional meetings of educators and education policy agencies. Each time I presented the work, I was asked unexpected questions that I had not previously considered. Each of these presentations pushed me back into the data collection and analysis with a new perspective. In this way the data were analyzed repeatedly, long before the process of organizing the data for the purpose of writing this book.

The Role of Serendipity

All good research projects start with a well-designed plan articulating research questions and laying out a data collection keyed to the questions. This planning is intended to minimize bias and ensure validity of findings. It requires the researcher to be clear about the purpose for each methodological decision and intentional in the steps taken toward answering questions. In the case of some studies—perhaps arguably more often among qualitative and even ethnographically influenced research—flexibility and reorientation along the way is an inherent part of the design. Data collection steps are dependent, in part, on the emergent findings of earlier steps. All of this rationally laid-out and articulated intention, however, omits the very real role played by serendipity in research projects such as this one.

An aptitude for making good discoveries through happy accidents played an important role in this research project. To exclude the role of serendipity from the methods is to fabricate a certainty of data, access, and even design that is disingenuous. Much of inductive research is messy and unpredictable—that is its strength as well as its challenge. Wading in to search for answers to questions, knowing the design plan has left room for adaptation is exciting but also daunting and at times disheartening. Identifying and seeking access to research sites, subjects, and data sources can be tidy and straightforward on paper, but the reality of implementation is frequently fraught with frustration and researcher doubt. The rewards of this sort of inquiry are many and worth the perseverance—because serendipity in research is not completely accidental.

Perseverance in the face of such doubts is more likely to put researchers in places where they are likely to meet people who can help, to seek places where information might be found, and to find doors that need to be opened. The well-placed researcher who is clear on research questions and operates with intent most often experiences the happy accident. Although serendipity arguably played a role numerous times in this research, there are four particular occasions that stand out as notable examples that occurred at pivotal moments of the research and had a most decisive influence on the direction of the project. Finding the question, discovering the data sources, and gaining entry and access to schools and teachers were all made possible through what was at least partially a serendipitous discovery, meeting, or door opening.

Although I first encountered the phenomena of OTTs while doing data collection in London for another project, I only decided to pursue the subject as a research project after returning to California. I recall the first lucky moment vividly, at an early morning breakfast meeting for local school district human resource directors. The regularly scheduled monthly meeting was a time they set aside to discuss shared concerns regarding staffing, the local labor market, changing policy and more. I was a guest there because I was collaborating with them on a regional workforce analysis. Not being noted for my eagerness to attend 6 a.m. breakfast meetings, it had taken a great deal of effort to finally decide to attend the meeting. It was there, however, that I learned, through an off-hand remark, about the practice of local school districts hiring teachers from the Philippines. One district HR director, in making his exit, remarked to another that he was off to Manila the following week on a recruitment trip. I marveled at the parallel, discussed it there, and drove away filled with questions. This breakfast lit the spark that became a multiyear focused research project.

Identifying the extent of teacher migration, however, proved difficult. None of the traditional sources of teacher and school data attended to it. Repeated web searches led me to an unlikely source. A website designed to allow disgruntled American job seekers a means of determining if the work position they desired had been offered to a foreign national guided me to the most important data source. The website used the Labor Condition Application data from the U.S. Department of Labor to ascertain which employers sought to hire foreign nationals with labor shortage visas and for which professions. I had never heard of an LCA, and a whole new set of analytical possibilities opened up.

My access to the California credential data on OTTs came about through a fortuitous seating arrangement at a Sacramento educational policy luncheon. Again, I had almost not attended as it felt like a distraction from the more pressing work of teaching and research. At the luncheon, I randomly sat next to the then-director of the California Commission on Teacher Credentialing. In chatting, as as is done at such gatherings, I mentioned my new research on overseas trained teachers and my frustrated efforts to determine countries of origin. It was then that the director commented that the commission collected this information in the teacher credentialing process though it had never done any systematic analysis of it. He offered to share it with me, and within a week I had seventeen years' worth of OTT California credentialing data.

Each of these two data obstacles was overcome in unexpected ways and only after a period of feeling thwarted and frustrated. My project frustration and related researcher doubt reached its peak, however, ten months after receiving funding for the qualitative data collection. My research plan was clear and well-articulated. I was supposed to be interviewing OTTs and doing case study research in schools—but unfortunately access was elusive. Six districts—major employers of OTTs—had granted me interviews with the human resource department but each had denied me school and teacher-level access. I had begun to doubt my ability to carry out the plan. Then District 7 granted me an interview with the human resource office. It was far away. The journey there and back would require an overnight stay, and I considered doing the interview by phone. Instead, I bundled my research assistant and myself into my car and made the journey. We optimistically brought enough clothes for a week.

That interview ended up being a major turning point in the study. The administrator herself wanted to know more about OTT experience. The district had been hiring overseas for seven years, and she was aware that the practice netted mixed results. The newest batch of Filipino teachers was arriving in the district in a few days. A group from Spain was already here and interviewing for posts. The administrator invited us to stay and observe their orientation. She connected us with continuing OTTs, opened doors to employing schools, and in general welcomed our inquiry and facilitated our access. What had started as a one-interview visit turned into a three-week field trip and a year-long data collection project. District 7 became the primary focal district because we went in person instead of talking on the phone, because one administrator shared our interest, because we persevered in seeking access when it seemed unlikely.

Serendipity plays an essential part in the unfolding of inductive research projects. Much can be planned in advance but other unforeseeable pieces and turns will unfold along with the inquiry. Researchers can and should take steps to create the optimal conditions for serendipity to play its role. Active participation in the field is essential. And by field, I mean both the research sites and the field of study. That Sacramento luncheon felt like a distraction at the time. I almost stayed away, yet attending that luncheon did more to further my research agenda than a day at my computer could possibly have achieved. Actively seeking research sites can be challenging and sometimes feel futile. Perseverance under doubt makes a serendipitous door opening much more likely. Clarity of intent, active engagement, and perseverance go far toward facilitating luck. Fortune will always play a part in what comes to pass, but we are not passive players in our fortune.

Moving Forward

More research is needed to better document the flow of teacher migrants into the United States and around the globe. Two main strands stand out as needing immediate attention. First, a more detailed national and international analysis of teacher migration flows is needed to more fully document the phenomenon and its changes over time. Second, the experience of sending countries, especially developing countries, needs to be studied in depth.

National and international teacher migration flow analysis requires better immigration and education data sources. In the United States, a teacher visa could greatly improve the access to relevant immigration data, permitting detailed information on date of entry, country of origin, length of stay, location of employment, and outcome of visa (home return, extension, emigration). Educational data should also include school-level and district-level reporting on temporarily employed overseas teachers. For example, the Institute of Education Science's annual National School and Staffing Survey should attend to OTT staffing patterns in schools. International data sources that make teacher migrations among other countries visible would also aid in making the process more transparent. UNESCO's annual teacher survey might, for example, attend to migration in its concern for nation-level teacher supply and demand. These and other sources of data must be identified before a more complete and ongoing migration scope and pattern analysis can be undertaken.

This study sought to understand the flows of migrant teachers into the United States from other countries. Yet, there is much more that needs to be looked at from the perspective of sending countries. Research into the experience of the Philippines, and other developing countries, would improve overall understanding and allow for more comprehensive policy recommendations around issues such as mitigating negative consequences, enacting international teacher credentialing, and facilitating reciprocal migration agreements. Increasingly, we are a globalized world with a mobile labor market. Planning for these movements, maximizing the benefits while minimizing the drawbacks, requires a global and international frame in research and policymaking.

NOTES

INTRODUCTION AND OVERVIEW

1. Teach For America (TFA) is a U.S.-based program that recruits recent American college graduates to teach in U.S. schools for two years. Modeled as a sort of domestic Peace Corps, TFA works to address educational inequity through the placement of talented, well-educated, young Americans into high-poverty classrooms. Small in overall scope, TFA has placed only 24,000 *corps members* since its inception in 1989.

2. Kingma (2006) discusses transnational nurse migration and documents how affluent countries have responded to nursing shortages by recruiting nurses from developing countries. She argues that nurse migration has negative consequences for developing countries as it depletes human resources from an already poor-to-marginal health care system.

3. "Teacher Recruitment, Retention, and Development Issues by the Commonwealth Secretariat" (paper presented at 15th Conference of Commonwealth Education Ministers, Session 7, Edinburgh, Scotland, October 29, 2003).

4. See the global monitoring report issued by UNESCO (2006).

5. See Educational International(2005).

6. In a study of the relationship between teacher certification and teacher effectiveness, Kane, Rockoff, and Staiger (2006) compared traditionally certified teachers with New York City teaching fellows and Teach for America corps members. They drew on six years of New York City student achievement data. Although "international" teachers were not the focus of their study, they did include teachers prepared overseas in their sample. The students of international teachers underperformed in relation to the students of the other teacher certification categories.

7. See Hutchison and Jazzar (2007).

8. Two teachers' union reports document the numbers of "foreign" and "international" teachers in U.S. schools. These reports, however, have been limited in number as well as scope. Although the union documentation of the number of teachers flowing into the United States is a useful insight into the size of the trend, these reports don't address the experience of schools and students.

163

1. THE SCOPE AND PATTERN OF
OVERSEAS TRAINED TEACHERS IN U.S. SCHOOLS

1. The U.S. Citizenship and Immigration Services explains the process: "The H-1C nonimmigrant temporary worker classification is for foreign nurses coming to the United States temporarily to perform services as a registered nurse in a health professional shortage area as determined by the Department of Labor (DOL)." Additional information is available at http://www.uscis.gov/portal/site /uscis/menuitem.eb1d4c2a3e5b9ac89243c6a7543f6d1a/?vgnextoid=fd980b8928 4a3210VgnVCM100000b92ca60aRCRD&vgnextchannel=fd980b89284a3210 VgnVCM100000b92ca60aRCRD.

2. US State Department details on J-1 visas: http://travel.state.gov/visa/temp /types/types_1267.html#1

3. U.S. Department of Labor overview of the H1B program: http://www .foreignlaborcert.doleta.gov/h-1b.cfm

4. One district already ran very close to the state percentage for qualified teachers.

5. See Prince George's County Public Schools, 2006–2007 Bridge to Excellence Master Plan, which describes progress toward meeting federal and state goals, retrieved from http://www1.pgcps.org/masterplan/index.aspx?id =7472.

6. It is important to note that for 13 percent (987) of OTTs the country of origin was not noted in the California Commission on Teacher Credentialing records.

2. THE PERFECT POLICY STORM

1. From an interview with a Filipina teacher in her second year of teaching in the United States. She was employed on an H1B visa.

2. Home salaries are based on the self-reported salaries of twenty-four Filipino teachers who were interviewed. Their monthly salaries ranged from a low of $200 U.S. dollars (equivalency) to a high of $600, with a median of $330 and a mean of $364. U.S. salaries are based on the self-reported annual salaries of twelve Filipino teachers with a low of $45,000, a high of $79,000, a median of $60,000 and a mean of $59,417.

3. See Karnow (1990, p. 197–209).

4. See Karnow (1990, pp. 200 and 207).

5. See Ceniza-Choy (2003) and Kingma (2006) for more on Filipino nurse migration.

6. See Parrenas (2008, p. 29).

7. This legislation is called the No Child Left Behind Act of 2001 even though it was officially signed into law in January 2002. States knew the content and expectations detailed in the act well before the final signing.

8. See Shulman (1987), Darling-Hammond (2000), and Rivkin, Hanushek, and Kain (2005).

9. See Shields et al. (2003).

10. See Cochran-Smith and Lytle (2006); Darling-Hammond and Young (2002); Nieto (2003); Sachs (2003); and Talbert-Johnson (2006).

11. See Shulman (1987) and Grossman (1990).

12. See Joe Mathews, The new import: Teachers, *Los Angeles Times,* August 10, 2002. Retrieved from http://articles.latimes.com/2002/aug/10/local/me-filipino10/3.

13. See Rita Villadiego, 60 Filipino teachers to lose jobs. *Inquirer News Service,* March 18, 2004. Retrieved from http://www.inquirer.net/.

14. Although the news article in n. 13 refers to the J-1 visa as a trainee visa, it is depicted by the U.S. government as a cultural exchange visa.

3. TRANSNATIONAL
TEACHER MOTIVATIONS AND PATHWAYS

1. In more recent labor market theory, the push-pull model has come to be seen as overly simplistic. A more complex frame of new theoretical perspectives has expanded it to account also for noneconomic motivations and complexities such as demography and family composition. For this reason, I prefer the terms *to* and *from* as they can encompass more than just issues such as wage differentials and yet follow well-established lines of migration study (Massey et al., 2008; Piore, 1979; Castles & Miller, 2009)

2. Four of the eight men are also parents. Without exception, the Filipino teacher parents had to leave their children in the Philippines for at least their first year in the United States.

3. There is also one case in the interview sample of a gay male OTT from Spain who became a teacher as a means of returning to the United States to be with his male partner. While not escaping social oppression in his home country, he was circumventing the social oppression that fails to recognize same-sex couples in marriage and immigration rights.

4. Although the teachers arrive in the United States with a district contract, in many districts that does not guarantee them a position. Typically, they then have to interview within the district in order to find a specific school and assignment. Teachers who do not get assignments may find themselves in the substitute pool or without a job. Most of the Filipino teachers accepted the first position offered. This was generally an offer made at a districtwide job fair of 10 to 15 minutes. The only exception to this was a consistent preference expressed by most Filipino teachers to work with Latino rather than African American students.

5. Most of the teachers did not have servants in the Philippines, and, as pointed out earlier in the chapter, they were barely making ends meet. The comment reflects more on the speaker's perception of the teachers' status in the United States than on any representation of their reality in the Philippines.

6. According to Marta, a male colleague left at Christmas of their first year. He was unhappy with the work and preferred to return to Spain.

7. Notably, teachers who arrived prior to 2002 reported paying significantly less in fees and expenses with none reporting more than $5,000. The

cost of migration increased substantially for Filipino teachers with the boom of 2002.

8. Several agency websites lay out this funding model, and we heard reports of it from teachers in California with friends teaching in other parts of the United States.

9. California's teacher skills and knowledge test known as the California Education Basic Skills Test—or as it is most commonly called, the CBEST.

10. See Lortie (1975).

11. Surge in foreign teachers fills gap but worries schools. *Sunday Star Times,* June 29, 2008.Retrieved from http://www.stuff.co.nz//510512.

12. For a discussion of teacher migration from South Africa to England, see Appleton (2006); McNamara, Lewis, and Howson (2006); Manik (2007); Miller (2007); Ochs (2003, 2005); De Villiers (2007); Manik, Maharaj, and Sookrajh (2006);and Manik (2010).

13. See McNamara, Lewis, and Howson (2007).

14. See Appleton, Sives, and Morgan (2006).

15. These international teacher labor market chutes and ladders are consistent with a trend in globalized nanny chains documented to advantage the middle class families of industrialized countries to the detriment of women and children in developing countries. In this trend, better-educated women of developing countries are recruited to care for the children of middle class families in industrialized countries. Parrenas (2001) describes the global care chain that commodofies care and advantages children with more "mothering" based on socioeconomic status. Hochschild (2000), drawing on Parrenas's work, characterizes this chain as a set of interdependent links between and within countries.

16. See Manik (2007, p. 62).

4. NAVIGATING MIGRATION

1. Even dishwashers in America make more money than teachers in the Philippines. Before US demand for Filipino teachers created migration opportunities, Nimuel considered looking for low skill work in the United States.

2. Many of the teachers from the Philippines reported having been "values" education teachers at home—a common subject taught there that covers morals and values from a religious and social position.

5. A TALE OF TWO SCHOOLS

1. See Liu and Moore-Johnson (2006).

2. See Dolton and Newson (2003).

3. See Villar and Strong (2007).

4. None of the Filipino teachers interviewed for this research were initially allowed to bring their families with them to the United States. The recruitment agencies that sponsored their J-1 visas made solo migration a condition of their sponsorship. After a year's employment, teachers could petition for permission to bring their children and spouse to join them. The agencies made a case-by-case

decision based on principal evaluations, teacher exam success (on state creden-tialing exams), and overall performance assessment. In contrast, all of the Spanish teachers sponsored by the California Department of Education were allowed to bring family with them from the point of arrival.

5. The National Council of Teachers of Mathematics issued the *Principles and Standards for School Mathematics* (2008), a report that makes teachers' math con-tent knowledge a top priority in improving students' math achievement. It can be found at http://standards.nctm.org. Another report, the 2007 *Trends in International Math and Science Study (TIMSS)* issued by the National Center for Education Statistics and found at http://nces.ed.gov/timss/index.asp, indicates that U.S. fourth and eighth grade students' math score are higher than the overall international average but still lower than those of students in top-achieving Asian and European countries with a wide achievement gap between U.S. white students and U.S. Latino and African American students. The report also indicates that American students are less likely than students elsewhere to be taught by teachers with a bachelor's or master's degree in mathematics—thereby highlighting the teacher content knowl-edge gap and leading many to call for increased teacher math education.

6. U.S. Department of Education, *Foundations for Success: Report of the National Mathematics Advisory Panel* (2008). Retrieved from http://www2.ed.gov/about/bdscomm/list/mathpanel/reports.html.

7. See Liu and Moore Johnson (2006).

8. See Smith and Ingersoll (2004).

9. See Little (1995, 2003) for a discussion of contested teacher leadership and implications for teachers' work.

10. See Dolton and Newson (2003).

6. TEACHERS' WORK

1. An interesting example of the past use of foreign-born teachers (although it is not known if they were foreign-trained) also illuminates the key roles teachers have historically played as community stalwarts, role models, and purveyors of cultural capital. In 1900, just over 6 percent of the nation's teachers were foreign-born. It is believed that these teachers were hired from their ethnic and religious communities of origin in order to transmit cultural and religious values from shared native roots, often working in private and parochial schools (Rury, 1989; Sanders, 1977). This is markedly different from the current OTT recruitment analyzed in this book. These modern movements specifically bring teachers from one country to teach in the low-status schools of another country, without atten-tion to cultural or ethnic match, in order to meet labor market needs.

2. See Massey (2008) and Piore (1979).

3. Reskin and Roos (1990) apply job queue theory primarily to explain gender inequity, but the theory has relevance to other patterns of labor and work distri-bution.

4. See Lortie (1975) for a discussion of the special but shadowed status of teaching work and Rury (1989) for a historical overview of the demographics and feminization of the teaching profession.

5. After World War II, the Bracero program intentionally restricted visas to low-skill or no-skill farm labor. Work requiring specific skills or knowledge was reserved for American workers. This had some interesting manifestations in the labor process. As farm work became increasingly mechanized so too did it also become increasingly Mexicanized. An account by Don Mitchel (in press) of lettuce harvesting in California's Monterey County discusses an excellent example of how a technical streamlining of production deskilled labor and increased the supply of Mexican Braceros in the fields. Prior to the early 1950s, lettuce was harvested then ice packed and processed in sheds by mostly American female skilled farm labor. Processing the lettuce took specialized knowledge of the treatment and packing of lettuce to ensure crispness and avoid core rot. In 1950, Braceros made up only 4 percent of Monterey's field labor—but the introduction of a field harvester changed all that. This new device could cool and package the lettuce automatically and then drop it onto delivery trucks to head to market. It essentially eliminated the need for shed workers and increased the demand for hard-working laborers to stoop for hours in hot fields picking the lettuce and placing them on the harvester's conveyer belts. It deskilled the labor of the lettuce harvest, and the need for Braceros boomed, and by 1955 Braceros accounted for 75 percent of Monterey's farm labor.

6. For a discussion of farm workers in the United States, see Hahamovitch (1997); Garcia (2001); Cohen (2011); and Mitchel (in press).

7. See Cohen (2011).

8. See Hahamovitch (2001).

9. The migration of female labor affects families differently than the migration of male labor. The temporary labor migration of women, especially mothers, alters the family structure and dynamic, creating new norms like Hochschild's (2000) nanny chain and altering the gendered labor of family life. Maternal and paternal roles are differently constructed in family life. When fathers migrate for family income, they are enacting established paternal expectations. When fathers, extended family members, and paid caregivers care for children left behind by migrating mothers, good mothering must be redefined from nurturer to provider if labor migration is to succeed.

When fathers and children do accompany their nurse wives and mothers—especially when the female nurse is also the primary family breadwinner—gender roles within the family may come under strain. At least in some families that migrated from India to the United States for female nursing work, it appears to have entrenched traditional gender roles within the family in order to assert cultural norms over the individual family constellation. In these cases, traditional gender norms are often asserted within the household in order to protect conventions and reify roles. In practice, this looks a great deal like women being primarily responsible for full-time wage work as well as full-time domestic labor while the frequently unemployed men seek community outlets for their energy and attention that will allow them to enact their traditional roles as patriarchs.

10. See George (2005).

11. See Hutchison and Jazzar (2007).

12. See Manik, Maharaj, and Sookrajh (2006).

13. For a discussion of the care aspects of teachers' work, see Nias (1981); Noddings (1992); Acker (1995); Nieto (2003); and Isenbarger and Zembylas (2006). Ladson-Billings (1995) makes the connection between a care orientation and teachers as bridges to cultural capital and opportunity.

14. See Meyer and Ramirez (2000) and DiMaggio and Powell (1983) for discussion of institutional isomorphism. In short, the theory proposes that through the process of isomorphism, institutions adopt similar structures and, as a result, closely resemble one another.

15. This argument was first made in Lora Bartlett and Judith Warren Little, The teacher workforce and problems of educational equity" (2011).

16. See Anderson-Levitt (2002).

17. See ibid., p. 10.

18. See Alexander (2001).

19. Delpit (1988) highlights the importance of teacher connection to students and community in achieving school success for students of color; Villegas and Lucas (2002) detail the need for culturally responsive pedagogical practice and teacher commitment to acting as agents of change in order to improve schooling outcomes for nondominant youth; and Cochran-Smith (1991) expands notions of teacher effectiveness to include particular knowledge, skills, and dispositions for reaching culturally diverse learners.

In a study of teacher distribution, Boyd, Lankford, Loeb, and Wyckoff (2005) found that teachers preferred to work in close proximity to where they went to school and were drawn to teach in schools that resembled schools they had attended. Furthermore, they argue that the "draw of home" disadvantages urban schools as they produce fewer teacher candidates. Similarly, Beauboeuf-LaFontant (1999) argues that desegregation policies profoundly influenced the composition of the teacher workforce because African-American teachers entered teaching in order to work within their communities with African-American students.

20. In a study of teacher distribution, Boyd, Lankford, Loeb, and Wyckoff (2005) found that teachers preferred to teach in close proximity to where they went to school and were drawn to teach in schools that resembled schools they had attended. Furthermore, they argue that the "draw of home" disadvantages urban schools as they produce fewer teacher candidates. Similarly, Beauboeuf-LaFontant (1999) argues that desegregation policies profoundly influenced the composition of the teacher work-force because African-American teachers entered teaching in order to work within their communities with African-American students.

21. See Alexandra Zavis and Tony Barboza, Teacher's suicide shocks school, *Los Angeles Times*, September 28, 2010. Retrieved from http://articles.latimes.com/2010/sep/28/local/la-me-south-gate-teacher-20100928.

22. See Christina Hoag, Rigoberta Ruelas, LAUSD Teacher Upset Over Low Ranking, Found Dead, *Huff Post Los Angeles*, September 27, 2010. Retrieved from http://www.huffingtonpost.com/2010/09/27/rigoberto-ruelas-lausd-te_n_740544.html.

23. See Cochran-Smith and Lytle (2006).

24. See Ladson-Billings (1990, 1995).

25. See Choe Sang-Hun, Teaching Machine Sticks to Script in South Korea, *New York Times*, July 10, 2010. Retrieved from http://www.nytimes.com /2010/07/11/science/11robotside.html. See also Audrey Watters, My Teacher is an Avatar, *KQED Mindshift*, April 11, 2011. Retrieved from http://mindshift.kqed .org/tag/engkey/; and http://singularityhub.com/2011/01/03/south-korea's-robot -teachers-to-test-telepresence-tools-in-the-new-year/: and Leslie Horn, South Korean Schools Testing Robot Teachers in *PCMag*, December 28, 2010. Retrieved from http://www.pcmag.com/article2/0,2817,2374800,00.asp ; and

26. See http://www.time.com/time/specials/packages/article/0,28804,202949 7_2030615_2029711,00.html #ixzz1QKvdxUHT

7. TRANSNATIONAL TEACHER MIGRATION

1. See Ingersoll and Smith (2004); Villar and Strong (2007); and Hutchinson and Jazzar (2007).

2. This particular way of describing the less savvy teacher—the less well-traveled and without personal contacts already in the United States—was heard so often in interviews that it came to feel like a refrain. The expectation these teachers held was that they would arrive in a promised land and all their problems would be addressed by the act of migration. Most of them then experienced a period of disillusionment and disappointment as the realities set in of living far from family, working in challenging school settings, and receiving few supports.

3. Home salaries are based on the self-reported salaries of twenty-four Filipino teachers in interviews. Their monthly salaries ranged from a low of $200 U.S. dollars (equivalency) to a high of $600, with a median of $330 and a mean of $364. U.S. salaries are based on the self-reported annual salaries of twelve Filipino teachers, with a low of $45,000, a high of $79,000, a median of $60,000, and a mean of $59,417.

4. International Summit on the Teaching Profession, March 16–17, 2011. Retrieved from http://www.oecd.org/dataoecd/62/8/47506177.pdf. See also Linda Darling Hammond, U.S. vs highest achieving nations. *Washington Post*, March 23, 2011. Retrieved from http://www.washingtonpost.com/blogs/answer-sheet/post /darling-hammond-us-vs-highest-achieving-nations-in-education/2011/03 /22/ABkNeaCB_blog.html.

AFTERWORD

1. For more information on the Maryland situation, see http://www.dol.gov /opa/media/press/whd/WHD20110357.htm

2. See *Francisco v. Oakland Unified School District*, case 3:2010cv04992, California Northern District Court, filed November 4, 2010. Retrieved from http://dockets.justia.com/docket/california/candce/3:2010cv04992/233785/; see also *Francisco v. Oakland Unified School District*, case RG10538648, Alameda County Courthouse. Retrieved from http://apps.alameda.courts.ca.gov/domainweb /service?CaseNbr=RG10538648&submitBtn=Submit&ServiceName=Domain

WebService&TemplateName=jsp%2Fcomplitcase.html&CurrBatchNbr=1; and Stephanie Rice, Teacher's fight to renew visa a first for Oakland, *San Francisco Chronicle*, June 18, 2011.Retrieved from http://www.sfgate.com/education /article/Teacher-s-fight-to-renew-visa-a-first-for-Oakland-2367736.php.

3. For more details on the registered nurse H1C visa program, see the U.S. Citizenship and Immigration Services website at http://www.uscis.gov/portal /site/uscis/menuitem.eb1d4c2a3e5b9ac89243c6a7543f6d1a/?vgnextoid=fd980b8 9284a3210VgnVCM100000b92ca60aRCRD&vgnextchannel=fd980b89284a32 10VgnVCM100000b92ca60aRCRD.

APPENDIX

1. http://www.ed-data.k12.ca.us/Pages/Home.aspx
2. See American Federation of Teachers (2009).
3. The Spanish teachers had a week-long orientation at a local university cosponsored by the state department of education. It took place prior to our research entry to the field. The teachers from Spain did not have a district-level orientation such as the one detailed here as experienced by the Filipino teachers.
4. Much was raised in that first week that would continue to be of concern to the Filipino teachers throughout their first year of teaching. Classroom management and how to teach in a much less hierarchical and teacher-centered pedagogical frame, teacher safety, earning respect of American colleagues, and gaining the trust of school administrators were all explicit topics. Less official but no less present were the off-line, between-session conversations about how to stay beyond the three-year visa, which teachers, if any, had managed to make that transition, and what it would take to achieve that goal.

REFERENCES

Acker, S. (1995). Carry on caring: The work of women teachers. *British Journal of Sociology of Education, 16*(1), 21–36.

Alexander, R. J. (2001). *Culture and pedagogy: International comparisons in primary education.* Oxford, England: Blackwell.

American Federation of Teachers. (2009). *Importing educators: Causes and consequences of international teacher recruitment.* Washington, DC.

Anderson-Levitt, K. M. (2002). *Teaching cultures: Knowledge for teaching first grade in France and the United States.* New York, NY: Hampton Press.

Appleton, S., Morgan, W., & Sives, A. (2006). Should teachers stay at home? The impact of international teacher mobility. *Journal of International Development, 18*(6), 771–786.

Appleton, S., Sives, A., & Morgan, W. (2006). The impact of international teacher migration on schooling in developing countries: The case of South Africa. *Globalization, Societies and Education, 4*(1), 121–142.

Barber, R. (2003). *Report to the national education association on trends in foreign teacher recruitment.* http://www.cwalocal4250.org/outsourcing/binarydata/foreignteacher.pdf Center for Economic Organizing.

Beauboeuf-LaFontant, T. (1999). A movement against and beyond boundaries: Politically relevant teaching among African-American teachers. *Teachers College Record, 100*(4), 702–723.

Borman, G., & Dowling, N. (2008). Teacher attrition and retention: A meta-analytic and narrative review of the research. *Review of Educational Research, 78*(3), 367.

Boyd, D., Lankford, H., Loeb, S., & Wyckoff, J. (2005). The draw of home: How teachers' preferences for proximity disadvantage urban schools. *Journal of Policy Analysis and Management, 24*(1), 113–132.

Castles, S., & Miller, M. J. (2009) *The age of migration: International population movements in the modern world.* New York: Guilford Press.

Choy, C. (2003). *Empire of care: Nursing and migration in Filipino American history.* Durham, NC: Duke University Press.

Cochran-Smith, M. (1991). Learning to teach against the grain. *Harvard Educational Review, 61*(3), 279–311.

Cochran-Smith, M., & Lytle, S. L. (2006). Troubling images of teaching in No Child Left Behind. *Harvard Education Review, 76*(4), 668–697.

Cohen, D. (2011). *Braceros: Migrant citizens and transnational subjects in the postwar United States and Mexico.* Chapel Hill, NC: University of North Carolina Press.

Commonwealth Secretariat, The. (2003). *Teacher recruitment, retention, and development issues.* Paper presented at the Fifteenth Conference of the Commonwealth Education Ministers, Edinburgh, Scotland.

Darling-Hammond, L. (2000). Teacher quality and student achievement. *Education Policy Analysis Archives, 8,* 1.

Darling-Hammond, L., Chung, R., & Frelow, F. (2002). Variation in teacher preparation: How well do different pathways prepare teachers to teach? *Journal of Teacher Education, 53*(4), 286–302.

Darling-Hammond, L., & Youngs, P. (2002). Defining "highly qualified teachers": What does "scientifically-based research actually tell us? *Educational Researcher, 31*(9), 13–25.

De Villiers, R. (2007). Migration from developing countries: The case of South African teachers to the United Kingdom. *Perspectives in Education, 25*(2), 67–76.

Delpit, L. (1988). The silenced dialogue: Power and pedagogy in teaching other people's children. *Harvard Educational Review, 56*(4), 379–385.

DiMaggio, P., & Powell, W. (1983). The iron cage revisited: Institutional isomorphism and collective rationality in organizational fields. *American Sociological Review, 48*(2), 147–160.

Dolton, P., & Newson, D. (2003). The relationship between teacher turnover and school performance. *London Review of Education, 1*(2), 132–140.

Educational International. (2005). Brain drain: Rich country seeks poor teachers. Brussels, Belgium.

Garcia, M. (2002). *A world of its own: Race, labor, and citrus in the making of greater Los Angeles, 1900–1970.* Chapel Hill, NC: University of North Carolina Press.

George, S. M. (2005). *When women come first: Gender and class in transnational migration.* Berkeley: University of California Press.

Gitlin, A., & Labaree, D. (1996). Historical notes on the barriers to the professionalization of American teachers: The influence of markets and patriarchy. In A. Hargreaves & I. Goodson (Eds.), *Teachers' professional lives* (pp. 88–108). London, England: Falmer Press.

Glass, G. V. (2008). Alternative certification of teachers. East Lansing, MI Great Lakes Center for Education Research & Practice.

Goe, L. (2002). Legislating equity: The distribution of emergency permit teachers in California. *Education Policy Analysis Archives, 10,* n42., 1–36.

Grant, G., & Murray, C. E. (1999) *Teaching in America: The slow revolution.* Cambridge, MA: Harvard University Press.

Grossman, P. (1990). *The making of a teacher: Teacher knowledge and teacher education.* New York: Teachers College Press.

Hahamovitch, C. (1997). *The fruits of their labor: Atlantic coast farmworkers and the making of migrant poverty, 1870–1945*. Chapel Hill, NC: University of North Carolina Press.

Hanushek, E. A., Kain, J. F., & Rivkin, S. G. (2004). The revolving door. *Education Next, 4*(1), 7.

Hochschild, A. (2000). The global nanny chain. *The American Prospect, 11*(4), 1–4.

Hutchison, C. B., & Jazzar, M. (2007). Mentors for teachers from outside the US. *Phi Delta Kappan, 88*(5), 368.

Ingersoll, R. (2001). Teacher turnover and teacher shortages: An organizational analysis. *American Education Research Journal, 38*(3), 499–534.

———. (2004). *Why do high-poverty schools have difficulty staffing their classrooms with qualified teachers?* Washington, DC: Center for American Progress and Institute for America's Future.

Ingersoll, R., & Smith, T. (2004). Do teacher induction and mentoring matter? *NASSP Bulletin, 88*(638), 28–40.

Isenbarger, L., & Zembylas, M. (2006). The emotional labour of caring in teaching. *Teaching and Teacher Education, 22*(1), 120–134.

Kane, T. J., Rockoff, J. E., & Staiger, D. O. (2006). What does certification tell us about teacher effectiveness? Evidence from New York City. Cambridge, MA: National Bureau of Economic Research.

Karnow, S. (1990). *In our image: America's empire in the Philippines*. New York, NY: Random House.

Kingma, M. (2006). *Nurses on the move: Migration and the global health care economy*. Ithaca, NY: ILR Press/Cornell University Press.

Laczko-Kerr, I., & Berliner, D. C. (2002). The effectiveness of Teach for America and other under-certified teachers on student academic achievement: A case of harmful public policy. *Education Policy Analysis Archives, 10*(37), 1–69.

Ladson-Billings, G. (1990). Like lightning in a bottle: Attempting to capture the pedagogical excellence of successful teachers of Black students. *International Journal of Qualitative Studies in Education, 3*(4), 335–344.

———. (1995). Toward a theory of culturally relevant pedagogy. *American Educational Research Journal, 32*(3), 465.

Little, J. W. (1995). Contested ground: The basis of teacher leadership in two restructuring high schools. *Elementary School Journal, 96*(1), 47–63.

———. (2003). Constructions of teacher leadership in three periods of policy and reform activism. *School Leadership and Management, 23*(4), 410–419.

Little, J. W., & Bartlett, L. (2010). The teacher workforce and problems of educational equity. *Review of Reseach in Education, 34*(1), 285.

Liu, E., & Johnson, S. M. (2006). New teachers' experiences of hiring: Late, rushed, and information-poor. *Educational Administration Quarterly, 42*(3), 324.

Lortie, D. (1975). *Schoolteacher: A sociological study*. Chicago, IL: University of Chicago Press.

Manik, S. (2007). To greener pastures: Transnational teacher migration from South Africa. *Perspectives in Education, 25*(2), 11.

Manik, S., Maharaj, B., & Sookrajh, R. (2006). Globalisation and transnational teachers: South African teacher migration to the UK. *Migracijske i etnicke teme, 22*(1–2), 15–33.

Massey, D., Arango, J., Hugo, G., Kouaouci. A., Pellegrino, A., Taylor, J. E. (2008). *Worlds in motion: Understanding international migration at the end of the millennium.* Oxford, England: Oxford University Press.

McNamara, O., Lewis, S., & Howson, J. (2007). "Turning the tap on and off": The recruitment of overseas trained teachers to the United Kingdom. *Perspectives in Education, 25*(2), 15.

Meyer, J., & Ramirez, F. O. (2000). The world institutionalization of education. In J. Schriewer (Ed.), *Discourse formation in comparative education,* Frankfurt, Germany: Peter Lang International Academic Publishers (pp. 111–132).

Miller, P. (2007). "Brain gain" in England: How overseas trained teachers have enriched and sustained English education. *Perspectives in Education, 25*(2), 25–37.

Mitchel, D. (in press). *They saved the crops: Migrant workers and the California landscape during the Bracero Era.* Athens: University of Georgia Press.

Nias, J. (1981). Commitment and motivation in primary school teachers. *Educational Review, 33*(3), 182–190.

Nieto, S. (2003a). Challenging current notions of "highly qualified teachers" through work in a teachers' inquiry group. *Journal of Teacher Education, 54*(5) 386–398.

———. (2003b). *What keeps teachers going?* New York: Teachers College Press.

Noddings, N. (1992). *The challenge to care in schools: An alternative approach to education.* New York: Teachers College Press.

Ochs, K. (2003). A summary of "teaching at risk": Teacher mobility and loss in Commonwealth member states. London, England: Commonwealth Secretariat.

———. (2005). *Report of a consultation the recruitment and migration of the highly skilled (nurses and teachers).* London, England: Social Transformation Programmes Division Commonwealth Secretariat.

Parrenas, R. S. (2001). *Servants of globalization: Women, migration, and domestic work.* Palo Alto, CA: Stanford University Press.

———. (2005). *Children of global migration.* Palo Alto, CA: Stanford University Press.

———. (2008). *The force of domesticity: Filipina migrants and globalization.* New York: NYU Press.

Piore, M. J. (1979) *Birds of passage: Migrant labor and industrial societies.* Cambridge, England: Cambridge University Press.

Reskin, B. F., & Roos, P. A. (1990). *Job queues, gender queues: Explaining women's inroads into male occupations.* Philadelphia, PA: Temple University Press.

Rivkin, S. G., Hanushek, E. A., & Kain, J. F. (2005). Teachers, schools, and academic achievement. *Econometrica, 73*(2), 417–458.

Rury, J. L. (1989). Who became teachers? The social characteristics of teachers in American history. In D. Warren (Ed.), *American teachers: Histories of a profession at work,* 9–48. New York: McMillan.

Sachs, J. (2003). Teacher professional standards: Controlling or developing teaching? *Teachers and Teaching, 9*(2), 175–186.

Sanders, J. (1977) *The education of an urban minority: Catholics in Chicago 1833–1965.* New York: Oxford University Press.

Shen, J. (1997). Teacher retention and attrition on public schools: Evidence from SASS91. *Journal of Educational Research, 91*(2).

Shields, P. M., Esch, C. E., Humphrey, D. C., Wechsler, M. E., Chang-Ross, C. M., Gallagher, H. A., et al. (2003). The status of the teaching profession 2003. Santa Cruz, CA: Center for Teaching and Learning.

Shulman, L. (1987). Knowledge and teaching: Foundations of the new reform. *Harvard Education Review, 57*(1), 1–23.

Stark, O. (1991) *The migration of labor.* Oxford, England: Blackwell.

Talbert-Johnson, C. (2006). Preparing highly qualified teacher candidates for urban schools: The importance of dispositions. *Education and Urban Society, 39*(1), 147–160.

UNESCO. (2006). Education for all: Global monitoring report. Paris, France: United Nations Educational, Scientific, and Cultural Organization.

Villar, A., & Strong, M. (2007). Is mentoring worth the money? A benefit-cost analysis and five-year rate of return of a comprehensive mentoring program for beginning teachers. *ERS Spectrum, 25*(3), 1–17.

Villegas, A. M., & Lucas, T. (2002). Preparing culturally responsive teachers: Rethinking the curriculum. *Journal of Teacher Education, 53*(1), 20.

ACKNOWLEDGMENTS

I believe in dynamic balance.

So often we juxtapose pieces of our lives as if they are in competition with one another. Work and home are positioned as the everlasting struggle between the professional and personal. Within the professional work of an academic, teaching and research are frequently framed as each questing for the same pool of time, energy, and intellect. Those who seek balance in these terms often draw on the metaphor of a two-pan scale, where balance requires the weight in one to be equal to the other and where one is always taking from the other.

In contrast, dynamic balance is the state of equilibrium in which centrifugal forces, due to a rotating mass, do not produce force. This is the sort of balance I see in my life. Research makes teaching possible and teaching makes research richer. My personal pursuits inform my professional interests and my professional interests lead me to new pursuits. Family, friends, and work all make one another possible. They are interdependent and all are in motion.

My family with whom I live—my children, Nathan, Rachel, and Fiona; my partner, James Burgess; and my father, Richard Bartlett—sustain me in this and all endeavors with their love and support. I appreciate the role their nourishment, patience, time, laughter, understanding, morning coffee deliveries, and limitless cups of mint tea played in keeping me centered and this project in focus.

I have the privilege of having many in my life whom I call both colleague and friend. These people believed in this research in its very first twinkling and stayed with me through to its final revision. Judith Warren Little and Ilana Horn each championed the research, my pursuit of new areas of teacher study, and me as a scholar. They listened to early analysis, read drafts, pushed my thinking, and were an ever-present and unparalleled source of intellectual and emotional support. In addition, many of my colleagues at U.C. Santa Cruz provided important feedback on the ideas and analysis in the book, most notably Rodney Ogawa, Doris Ash, Steve McKay, and Greta Gibson.

Alisun Thompson was the best possible graduate student researcher to work with me on this research. I met her just as this project began, and she participated in all stages of the data collection and analysis. She is a dedicated, intelligent, and insightful researcher and scholar. The project benefited tremendously from her engagement with it. I am proud and fortunate to call her my advisee, my colleague, and my friend.

Other graduate students also contributed to this work. Bill Zahner, now an assistant professor at Boston University, was instrumental in creating the maps while a PhD student at U.C. Santa Cruz. Priya Diaz assisted with early data organization, and Yolanda Diaz listened to and gave feedback on early analysis and framing. All of the students in my qualitative methods classes for the past five years heard various aspects of the work as I drew on it in my teaching. The role they played as intelligent critical students gave the work an important early audience.

I have many further allies who fill my life with friendship, love, critical mirrors, detailed feedback, edits, ideas, air, and hope depending on the day and its need. Ann Reale, Jason Wallace, Rheanna Bates, Arwen Swink, John Nuhn, Elizabeth Duff, Melinda Bartlett Blante, Lorilyn Parmer Folks, Jen Angel, Michael McColl, Monica Vantoch, Lorien Wood, Peter Cornelius, Mason Cornelius, and Rachel Rosenfeld all played important roles in sustaining me and this project throughout its many ages and stages. I am fortunate to have more allies than space allows for name-by-name acknowledgment. Thank you.

This research and book owe much to the funders who made data collection possible and the editor who recognized the importance of the topic and helped me to shape a compelling book. The University of California's Labor Employment Research Fund and a private foundation's domestic public policy fellowship funded all of the data collection. The Atlantic Public Policy Fellowship, awarded by the British Council, made discovery of the topic possible. Elizabeth Knoll is the editor every author deserves. She offered equal parts confidence in me, interest in the book topic, and an insistence on well-crafted prose in a clear and articulate voice. She served as both guide and critic in the book writing process, eliciting from me a much better book than would have resulted without her.

Most important, this book would not have been possible without the teachers who shared their stories with and the schools that opened their doors to me. This is their story. I have the privilege of having been allowed to bear witness to their experience and been permitted to share the collective tale. I respect the courage it took for them to share their stories, and I appreciate the confidence they instilled in me in granting me that opportunity. I hope that the result is increased understanding of the experience of teacher migration and improvements in the lived experiences of teachers, students, and public schools.

I am grateful for the people and projects that dynamically balance my life and work with a diversity of purpose and pleasure. Thank you.

INDEX

Students: attention of, 1–2; expectations, 77; IEPs, 78–79; feedback, 79; achievement and OTT turnover, 84; tracks at New Urban High School, 86; of Central High School, 89, 91, 92–93; behavior, 89–90, 111; cultural differences of U.S., 89–90, 111–112; teacher interaction with, 89–90; achievement and teacher quality, 91; of New Urban High School, 91–93; teachers' cultural affinity and, 111–112, 117
Sunder, Preetha, 49–50
Suzrez, Clara, 74

Taft, William, 34
Taft Commission, 34
Teacher education, 15, 73–74
Teacher migration, 5–8; Philippines, 8; into U.S., 8–9; motivation of, 10, 41, 45–49, 123; dilemmas of, 11; colonization and, 34–35; migrating *to*, 46, 51–57, 82, 118, 138–139; salary and, 46–49, 64, 68–69, 72; migrating *from*, 46–51, 81, 82–84, 87, 90, 118; marriage and, 49–50, 53–54; social oppression and, 49–50; costs of, 58, 60–61, 87, 90, 128; self-guided, 58; advertisements for, 66; initiating, 66; positioning for, 66–67; teaching as reason for, 67–68; marketability and, 68; teacher quality and, 68; risks of, 72–73; career plans and, 75; mass movements, 103; labor queues and, 103–105; patterns, 104, 140, 141–146; nursing migration and, 108–110; trend of, 110; teaching profession, 122–123; industrialized countries and, 123–125; international, 137; scale of, 140, 141–146; tracking, 140; flow of, 160–161. *See also* Short-term teacher migration
Teacher migration pathways, 91–92; individual migration, 57–58; formal government programs, 58–59; recruitment agencies, 59–61, 88; implications of, 61–64; chutes and ladders, 62
Teacher quality: NCLB and, 36–37, 60, 100, 105, 114–115, 128–129, 140; migration and, 68; Filipino teachers, 88;

student achievement and, 91; definition of, 128; school capacity and, 129
Teachers: qualifications of, 3; specialization, 10, 32, 66, 113; work of, 11; credentialing process, 15, 70, 105, 121; nationality, 15; distribution of, 16, 36, 64, 122; credential data in California, 23, 25–26, 145–146; LCA certified, 23; in Philippines, American, 35; educational policy and qualifications of, 36–37; subject knowledge of, 37, 58; living abroad, 54; testing of, 58, 71; labor markets, 62, 127, 139; demand for, 66; loyalty, 77; workforce of, 83, 138; student interaction with, 89–90; effectiveness, 91, 113–114; organization for work of, 94–99, 125; retention, 95, 119, 135; screening, 95; job preview, 95–96; supports, new, 96–97, 109; globalization, 103, 139; movement of, 103; definition of, 103–104; as guest workers, 105–110, 118; narrowing work of, 110–114, 121; skills of, 111; cultural affinity, 111–112, 117; as role models, 113; ratings, 113–114; online, 116; robot, 116; transplanting, 119–120; status of, 124, 133; layoffs, 127; visas, 129–130, 134–136; retaining effective, 135; rights of, 136. *See also* Filipino teachers; Highly qualified teachers; Overseas trained teacher
Teach For America (TFA), 3, 121
Teaching: community and, 112–113; relational aspects of, 112–114, 117; culture and, 115–116; definition of, 116; online, 116; profession, 122–123
Tenure, 80, 133
Texas: OTTs in, 19; LCAs in, 21; school districts of, 21
TFA. *See* Teach For America
Thomas, David, 98
Thompson, Alisun, 148, 156
Time, 116
Torrez, Faith, 70
Transient schools, 82, 119, 120; OTTs and, 10–11, 83, 99–100; academic achievement of, 84; hiring process of,